DAY HIKES AROUND
Los Angeles

82 GREAT HIKES

Robert Stone

4th EDITION

Day Hike Books, Inc.
RED LODGE, MONTANA

Published by Day Hike Books, Inc.
P.O. Box 865
Red Lodge, Montana 59068

Distributed by The Globe Pequot Press
246 Goose Lane
P.O. Box 480
Guilford, CT 06437-0480
800-243-0495 (direct order) · 800-820-2329 (fax order)
www.globe-pequot.com

Photographs by Robert Stone
Design by Paula Doherty

The author has made every attempt to provide accurate information in this book. However, trail routes and features may change—please use common sense and forethought, and be mindful of your own capabilities. Let this book guide you, but be aware that each hiker assumes responsibility for their own safety. The author and publisher do not assume any responsibility for loss, damage or injury caused through the use of this book.

Cover photo: Newton Canyon Falls, Hike 17
Back cover photo: Chicken Ridge Bridge between
Rustic and Rivas Canyons, HIke 51

Table of Contents

Malibu Canyon to Beverly Hills

About the Hikes
and the Los Angeles area

Despite the imminent presence of the Los Angeles metropolis, there are thousands of acres of natural, undeveloped land with countless out-of-the-way hiking trails. This guide includes 82 day hikes within a 50-mile radius of the city. Most hikes are found on local, state, and national land; wilderness areas; and within the expansive Santa Monica Mountains National Recreation Area. The trails have been chosen for their scenery and variety and include a range of difficulty levels, providing access to the green areas in the metropolitan area.

An overall map on the next page identifies the general locations of the hikes and major roads. Four area maps, as noted on this map, provide additional details.

Each hike also includes its own map, a summary, driving and hiking directions, and an overview of distance/time/elevation. Relevant maps, including U.S.G.S. topographic maps, are listed with each hike if you wish to explore more of the area. A quick glance at the hikes' summaries will allow you to choose a hike that is appropriate to your ability and desire.

A few basic necessities will make your hike more enjoyable. Wear supportive, comfortable hiking shoes. Take along hats, sunscreen, sunglasses, drinking water, snacks, and appropriate outerwear. Poison oak and ticks are common. Exercise caution by using insect repellent and staying on the trails.

Coastal Region of the Santa Monica Mountains

Hikes 1—61 are found along the Pacific Coast and among the foothills, canyons, and peaks of the Santa Monica Mountains. This range extends roughly 46 miles east and west parallel to the coast, from downtown Los Angeles to Point Mugu. The mountains are 8—12 miles wide and lie along the San Andreas Fault. Elevations range from sea level to 3,111 feet at Sandstone Peak.

The trails meander along the coastal foothills, traverse peaks and ridges, and drop down across the northern side of the range facing into the rolling landscape of interior California. Highlights of the hikes include panoramic views from the ocean to the city, unusual geological formations and rock outcroppings, waterfalls, cliff overlooks, ridge walks, canyons, old ranch roads (including Ronald Reagan's ranch), filming locations, and cool shady retreats. Many state parks have been established in this region, including the expansive Point Mugu, Malibu Creek, and Topanga state parks. Beaches and coastal communities are scattered along the Pacific Coast Highway (Highway 1), the access road to most of these hikes.

The mountain's best known trail is the Backbone Trail. It extends approximately 64 miles across ridges and canyons on a nearly continuous trail, linking the Santa Monica Mountains from east to west. Several hikes include segments of this trail.

Hollywood Hills and Griffith Park

Hollywood Hills and Griffith Park sit at the east end of the Santa Monica Mountain Range. Eleven hikes (62—73) are located in this area, just minutes from downtown Los Angeles. Griffith Park, the largest municipal park in the United States, has both tourist attractions and solitary retreats within its 4,100 acres. The rugged urban wilderness contains a 53-mile network of hiking and equestrian trails through semi-arid foothills, oak groves, and wooded glens. The mountains and steep interior canyons of the Hollywood Hills are largely undeveloped and offer a haven for humans and animals in the midst of Los Angeles.

Highlights of these hikes include overlooks of the city, secluded canyons, gardens, the Hollywood Reservoir, Griffith Park Observatory and Planetarium, a 1926 merry-go-round, and a hike up to the famous "HOLLYWOOD" sign. Several other local attractions are within easy access, such as the Los Angeles Zoo, Gene Autry Western Heritage Museum, Travel Town Museum, and five golf courses.

(The Venice Canals, Hike 74, are six interwoven water canals just south of Santa Monica. Around the canals are landscaped walkways and diverse architecture.)

Palos Verdes Peninsula

The last eight hikes (75—82) are scattered along the coast of the Palos Verdes Peninsula at the southernmost point of Los Angeles County. This geographically interesting area includes oceanside cliffs, beaches, coves, grassy bluffs, actively slipping landslides, and some of the best tidepools in the area. A beautiful lighthouse sits at the tip of Point Fermin. Sunken City, also at Point Fermin, is a surreal uninhabited landscape of house foundations and chimneys that continue to slide closer to the ocean.

These hikes will undoubtedly give you a greater appreciation of Los Angeles. Enjoy your time out on the trails!

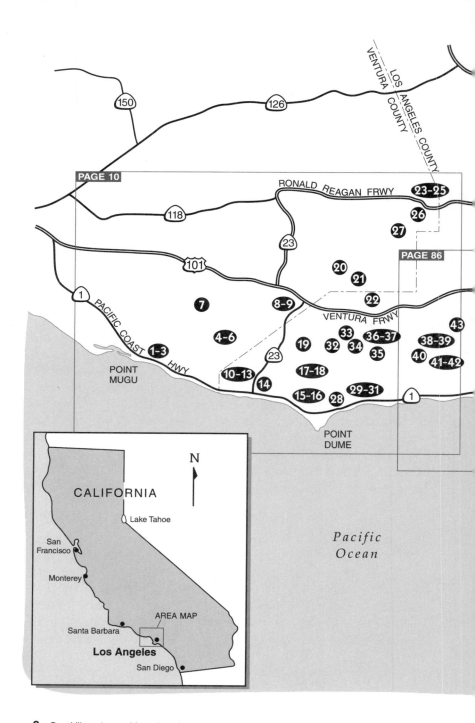

PAGE 10

150

126

LOS ANGELES COUNTY
VENTURA COUNTY

RONALD REAGAN FRWY

23-25

26

27

118

23

20

21

PAGE 86

101

1

PACIFIC COAST

7

8-9

22

VENTURA FRWY

43

4-6

33

36-37

38-39

1-3

HWY

19

32

34

35

40

41-42

POINT
MUGU

23

17-18

10-13

14

15-16

28

29-31

1

POINT
DUME

N

CALIFORNIA

Lake Tahoe

San
Francisco

Monterey

Pacific
Ocean

AREA MAP

Santa Barbara

Los Angeles

San Diego

MAP OF THE HIKES

LOS ANGELES and VICINITY

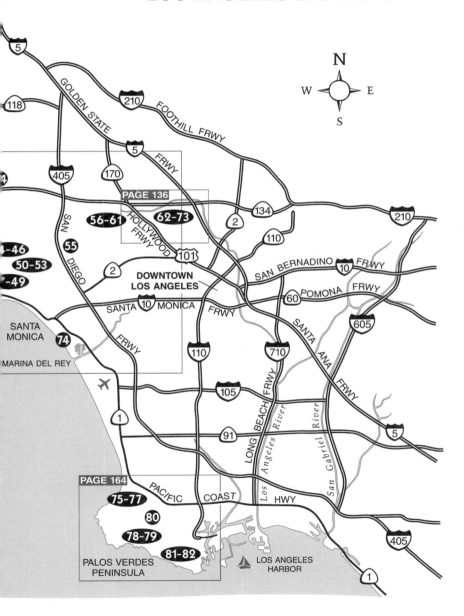

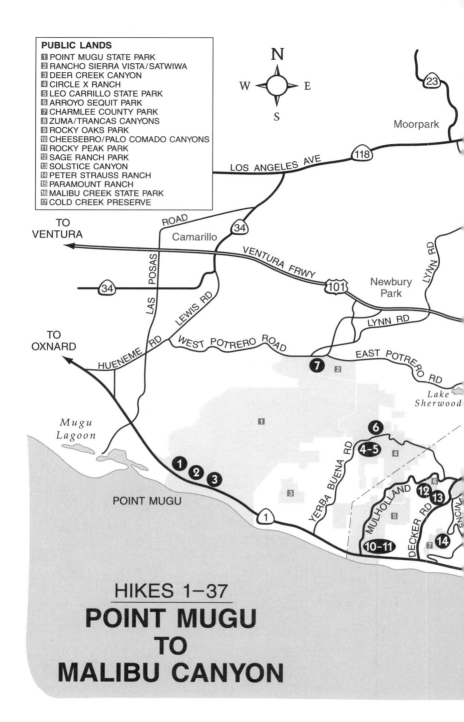

PUBLIC LANDS
1. POINT MUGU STATE PARK
2. RANCHO SIERRA VISTA/SATWIWA
3. DEER CREEK CANYON
4. CIRCLE X RANCH
5. LEO CARRILLO STATE PARK
6. ARROYO SEQUIT PARK
7. CHARMLEE COUNTY PARK
8. ZUMA/TRANCAS CANYONS
9. ROCKY OAKS PARK
10. CHEESEBRO/PALO COMADO CANYONS
11. ROCKY PEAK PARK
12. SAGE RANCH PARK
13. SOLSTICE CANYON
14. PETER STRAUSS RANCH
15. PARAMOUNT RANCH
16. MALIBU CREEK STATE PARK
17. COLD CREEK PRESERVE

N
W E
S

Moorpark

LOS ANGELES AVE 118

ROAD

TO VENTURA

Camarillo 34

VENTURA FRWY

LAS POSAS RD

LEWIS RD

34

101 Newbury Park

LYNN RD

LYNN RD

TO OXNARD

HUENEME RD

WEST POTRERO ROAD

EAST POTRERO RD

7 2

Lake Sherwood

Mugu Lagoon

1

6

YERBA BUENA RD

4-5

4

POINT MUGU

1 2 3

3

MULHOLLAND

12

13

DECKER RD

6

5

1

10-11

7

14

ENCINAL

HIKES 1–37
POINT MUGU
TO
MALIBU CANYON

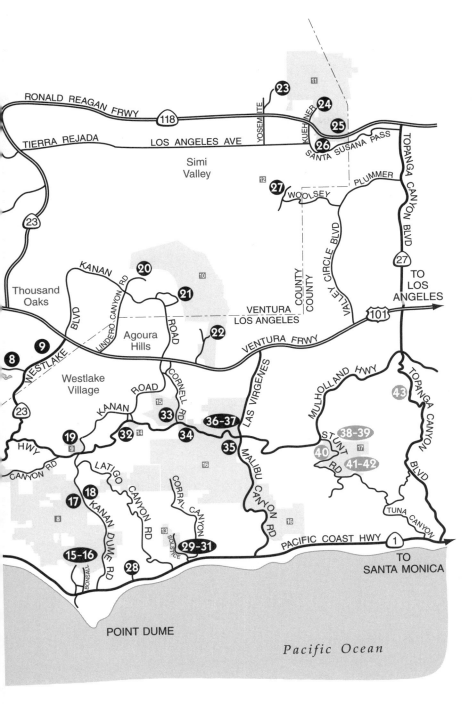

Hike 1
Chumash Trail—Mugu Peak Loop
POINT MUGU STATE PARK

Hiking distance: 4.5 mile loop
Hiking time: 2.5 hours
Elevation gain: 1,100 feet
Maps: U.S.G.S. Point Mugu
Santa Monica Mountains West Trail Map

map
next page

Summary of hike: La Jolla Valley Natural Preserve is an expansive high-mountain valley at the far western end of the Santa Monica Mountains. The oak-studded grassland rests 800 feet above the ocean at the foot of Mugu Peak. The high ridges of Laguna Peak, La Jolla Peak, and the serrated Boney Mountain ridgeline surround the rolling meadow. La Jolla Valley can be accessed from La Jolla Canyon (Hike 2), Big Sycamore Canyon (Hike 7), and the Chumash Trail (this hike), the steepest and most direct route. For centuries, this trail was a Chumash Indian route connecting their coastal village at Mugu Lagoon with La Jolla Valley. This hike steeply ascends the coastal slope on the west flank of Mugu Peak. The elevated Mugu Peak Trail circles the mountain slope below the double peak, with sweeping ocean and mountain vistas.

Driving directions: From Santa Monica, drive 35 miles northbound on the Pacific Coast Highway/Highway 1 to the large parking pullout on the right, across from the Navy Rifle Range and Mugu Lagoon. (The trailhead parking area is 16.8 miles past Kanan Dume Road in Malibu and 3.5 miles west of the well-marked Sycamore Canyon.)

Heading southbound on the Pacific Coast Highway/Highway 1 from Las Posas Road in southeast Oxnard, drive 2.3 miles to the parking area on the left by the posted trailhead.

Hiking directions: Begin climbing up the chaparral and cactus covered hillside, gaining elevation with every step. At a half mile, the trail temporarily levels out on a plateau with sweeping coastal views, including the Channel Islands. The steadily ascending trail gains 900 feet in 0.7 miles to a T-junction on a saddle. Begin the loop to the left, crossing over the saddle into the vast La Jolla Valley. The valley is surrounded by rounded mountain peaks, the jagged Boney Mountain ridge, and the surrealistic Navy radar towers by Laguna Peak. Cross the open expanse to a posted junction with the La Jolla Valley Loop Trail at 1.2 miles. Take the right fork and head southeast across the meadow on a slight downward slope. Drop into an oak woodland and cross a stream. Parallel the stream through a small draw to a another junction. Take the right fork 100 yards to a path on the right by an old circular metal tank. Bear right on the Mugu Peak Trail and cross the creek. Traverse the hillside to the west edge of La Jolla Canyon. Follow the ridge south on the oceanfront cliffs. Wind along the south flank of Mugu Peak, following the contours of the mountain to a trail split on a saddle between the mountain's double peaks. The right fork ascends the rounded grassy summit. Veer left, hiking along the steep hillside to the west side of the peak. Cross another saddle and complete the loop. Return down the mountain to the trailhead.

Hike 2
La Jolla Valley Loop from La Jolla Canyon
POINT MUGU STATE PARK

Hiking distance: 6 miles round trip
Hiking time: 3 hours
Elevation gain: 750 feet
Maps: U.S.G.S. Point Mugu
        Santa Monica Mountains West Trail Map

map
next page

Summary of hike: La Jolla Canyon is a narrow, steep gorge with a perennial stream and a 15-foot waterfall. The canyon leads up to La Jolla Valley Natural Preserve at an 800-foot elevation, a broad valley with rolling grasslands at the west end of the Santa Monica Mountains. Mugu Peak, La Jolla Peak, and Laguna Peak surround the oak-dotted meadow. This hike climbs through the rock-walled canyon and loops around the meadow to a coastal overlook and a pond with a picnic area.

Driving directions: From Santa Monica, drive 33 miles northbound on the Pacific Coast Highway/Highway 1 to the posted La Jolla Canyon entrance on the right. (The trailhead entrance is 15 miles past Kanan Dume Road in Malibu and 1.6 miles west of the well-marked Sycamore Canyon.)

Heading southbound on the Pacific Coast Highway/Highway 1 from Las Posas Road in southeast Oxnard, drive 4.2 miles to the entrance on the left.

Hiking directions: From the north end of the parking lot, at the Ray Miller Trailhead, take the La Jolla Canyon Trail north. Follow the wide path up the canyon, crossing the stream several times. The third crossing is just below a beautiful 15-foot waterfall and a pool surrounded by large boulders. Natural rock steps lead up to the top of the falls. Continue along the east side of the canyon, passing large sandstone rocks and caves. At a gorge, the trail sharply doubles back to the right, leading up the side of the canyon. At 1.2 miles, take the left fork towards Mugu Peak. Cross the stream and head southwest to a ridge above La Jolla Canyon and the ocean. The trail levels out and passes two trail junctions. Stay to the right both times, heading north across the rolling grassland. At 2.7 miles the trail joins the wide La Jolla Valley Loop Trail—head to the right. As you near the mountains of La Jolla Canyon, take the first cutoff trail to the right, leading past the pond and rejoining the La Jolla Canyon Trail. Head to the right, and go two miles down canyon, returning to the trailhead.

TO
OXNARD

Mugu Lagoon

HIKES 1–2
LA JOLLA VALLEY
MUGU PEAK
POINT MUGU STATE PARK

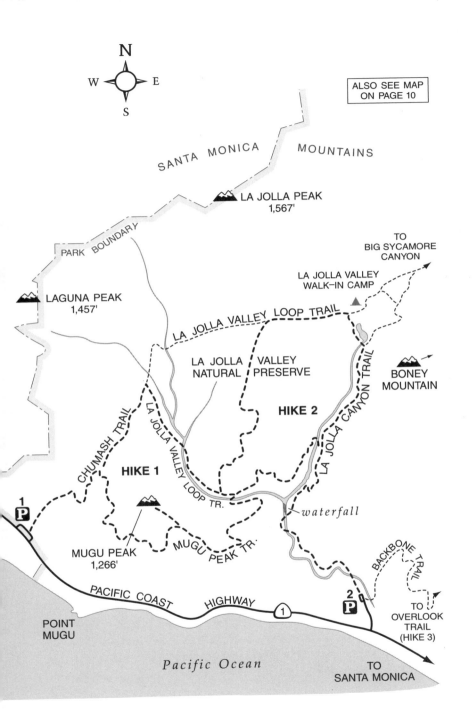

N
W E
S

ALSO SEE MAP
ON PAGE 10

SANTA MONICA MOUNTAINS

LA JOLLA PEAK
1,567'

PARK BOUNDARY

TO
BIG SYCAMORE
CANYON

LA JOLLA VALLEY
WALK–IN CAMP

LAGUNA PEAK
1,457'

LA JOLLA VALLEY LOOP TRAIL

LA JOLLA
NATURAL VALLEY PRESERVE

BONEY
MOUNTAIN

CHUMASH TRAIL

LA JOLLA VALLEY LOOP TR.

HIKE 2

LA JOLLA CANYON TRAIL

HIKE 1

1
P

MUGU PEAK
1,266'

MUGU PEAK TR.

waterfall

BACKBONE TRAIL

PACIFIC COAST HIGHWAY

1

2
P

TO
OVERLOOK
TRAIL
(HIKE 3)

POINT
MUGU

Pacific Ocean

TO
SANTA MONICA

Hike 3
Scenic and Overlook Trails Loop
POINT MUGU STATE PARK

Hiking distance: 2 mile loop
Hiking time: 1 hour
Elevation gain: 900 feet
Maps: U.S.G.S. Point Mugu
       Santa Monica Mountains West Trail Map

Summary of hike: The Scenic and Overlook Trails are located along the coastal frontage of Point Mugu State Park. The trail follows the ridge separating Big Sycamore Canyon from La Jolla Canyon. This short but beautiful hike climbs up the chaparral-covered ridge to several panoramic overlooks of the Pacific Ocean.

Driving directions: From Santa Monica, drive 31 miles northbound on the Pacific Coast Highway/Highway 1 to the posted Big Sycamore Canyon entrance on the right. (The trailhead entrance is 13.3 miles past Kanan Dume Road in Malibu and 5.3 miles west of the well-marked Leo Carrillo State Beach.) Turn right and park in the day-use pay parking lot 0.1 mile ahead on the left. (Parking is free in the pullouts along the PCH.)

Heading southbound on the Pacific Coast Highway/Highway 1 from Las Posas Road in southeast Oxnard, drive 5.8 miles to the Point Mugu State Park entrance on the left.

Hiking directions: From the parking area, walk up the road past the campground to the Big Sycamore Canyon trailhead gate. Continue up the unpaved road about 50 yards to the signed junction with the Scenic Trail. Take the trail to the left (west) across Big Sycamore Creek, and head up the wooden steps. The trail steadily gains elevation up an open, grassy hillside with good canyon views. At the saddle near the top of the hill is a trail split. The left fork leads a short distance to an ocean overlook. Continue up to several more viewpoints. Return back to the junction, and head north to a junction with the Overlook Trail. Take this service road downhill to the right, winding 0.9 miles back to the Big Sycamore Canyon floor. Near the bottom, a series of five gentle switchbacks lead to the junction. Take the canyon trail to the right, leading 0.4 miles back to the trailhead gate.

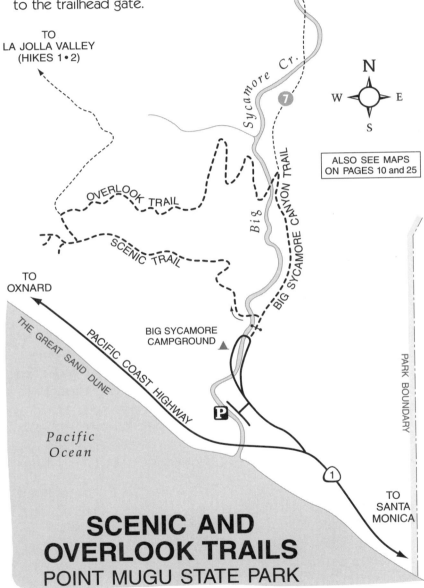

TO
LA JOLLA VALLEY
(HIKES 1 • 2)

Sycamore Cr.

7

N
W — E
S

ALSO SEE MAPS
ON PAGES 10 and 25

OVERLOOK TRAIL

SCENIC TRAIL

Big

BIG SYCAMORE CANYON TRAIL

TO
OXNARD

THE GREAT SAND DUNE

PACIFIC COAST HIGHWAY

BIG SYCAMORE
CAMPGROUND

P

Pacific
Ocean

PARK BOUNDARY

1

TO
SANTA
MONICA

SCENIC AND
OVERLOOK TRAILS
POINT MUGU STATE PARK

Hike 4
Grotto Trail
CIRCLE X RANCH

Hiking distance: 3.5 miles round trip
Hiking time: 2 hours
Elevation gain: 650 feet
Maps: U.S.G.S. Triunfo Pass
        Santa Monica Mountains West Trail Map
        N.P.S. Circle X Ranch Site

Summary of hike: The Grotto Trail is located in the 1,655-acre Circle X Ranch bordering Point Mugu State Park. Once a Boy Scout wilderness retreat, the Circle X Ranch is now a national park and recreation area. The Grotto, at the end of this trail, is a maze of large, volcanic boulders in a sheer, narrow gorge formed from landslides. The West Fork of the Arroyo Sequit flows through the caves and caverns of The Grotto, creating cascades and pools.

Driving directions: From the Pacific Coast Highway/Highway 1 in Santa Monica, drive 38 miles northbound to Yerba Buena Road and turn right. (Yerba Buena Road is 10.1 miles past Kanan Dume Road and 2 miles past Leo Carrillo State Beach.) Continue 5.3 miles up the winding road to the Circle X Ranger Station on the right. Park by the ranger station, or continue 0.2 miles downhill to the day-use parking area, just past the posted Grotto Trailhead.

From the Pacific Coast Highway/Highway 1 and Las Posas Road in southeast Oxnard, drive 9 miles southbound to Yerba Buena Road (3.3 miles past Big Sycamore Canyon) and follow the directions above.

Hiking directions: From the ranger station, walk 0.2 miles down the unpaved road to the posted Grotto trailhead, just before reaching the lower parking area. Continue downhill, crossing the West Fork of Arroyo Sequit. At 0.4 miles, the trail passes the Canyon View Trail (Hike 5) and recrosses the creek at a 30-foot waterfall. After crossing, curve left, traversing a grassy ridge. Descend to the canyon floor where the trail joins the Happy Hollow Campground Road at 1.2 miles. Follow the road to the left into a primitive campground and cross the creek, picking up the posted Grotto Trail again. Head downstream to a bridge that crosses the creek into the Happy Hollow Campground. Instead of crossing the bridge, continue straight ahead and cross the creek by a pumphouse. Follow the creek a few hundred feet to The Grotto.

After exploring The Grotto, return to the bridge that accesses the campground. Walk through the campground to the road and bear to the right. Follow the winding road, and rejoin the Grotto Trail on the left. Retrace your steps to the parking lot.

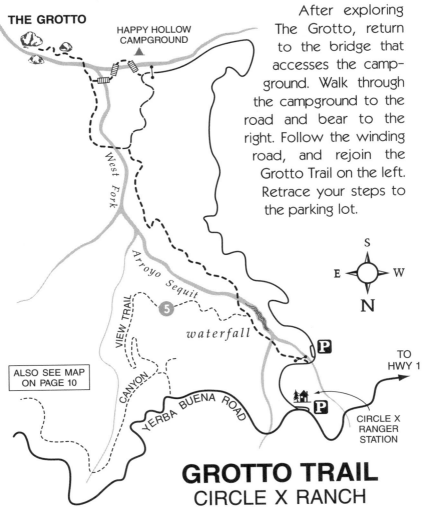

THE GROTTO

HAPPY HOLLOW CAMPGROUND

West Fork

Arroyo Sequit

VIEW TRAIL

5

waterfall

CANYON

ALSO SEE MAP ON PAGE 10

YERBA BUENA ROAD

S

E — W

N

P

TO HWY 1

P

CIRCLE X RANGER STATION

GROTTO TRAIL
CIRCLE X RANCH

Hike 5
Canyon View—
Yerba Buena Road Loop
CIRCLE X RANCH

Hiking distance: 3.2 mile loop
Hiking time: 1.5 hours
Elevation gain: 500 feet
Maps: U.S.G.S. Triunfo Pass
Santa Monica Mountains West Trail Map
N.P.S. Circle X Ranch Site

Summary of hike: Circle X Ranch sits below Boney Mountain in the upper canyons of Arroyo Sequit. The Canyon View Trail traverses the brushy hillside of the deep, east-facing canyon. The panoramic views extend down the canyon to the Pacific Ocean. The northern views reach the jagged Boney Mountain ridge and the 3,111-foot Sandstone Peak, the highest peak in the Santa Monica Mountains. The trail connects the Grotto Trail (Hike 4) with the Backbone Trail (Hike 6).

Driving directions: Same as Hike 4.

Hiking directions: From the ranger station, walk 0.2 miles down the unpaved road to the posted Grotto Trailhead, just before reaching the lower parking area. Pass the trail gate and follow the dirt road past a picnic area to another trail sign. Take the footpath downhill and cross the West Fork Arroyo Creek. Parallel the east side of the creek to a signed junction. (Twenty yards to the right is a waterfall—Hike 4.) Bear left on the Canyon View Trail, and traverse the canyon wall, following the contours of the mountain. Climb two switchbacks to a junction. For a shorter 1.5-mile loop, take the Connector Trail 100 yards to the left, reaching Yerba Buena Road, and return 0.35 miles to the ranger station. For this longer hike, stay to the right and cross a rocky wash. Head up the hillside to a south view down canyon to the ocean and the Channel Islands and a north view of the Boney Mountain ridge. Continue to Yerba Buena Road, across from the Backbone Trail (Hike 6). Return to the left on Yerba Buena Road, and walk 1.1 mile back to the trailhead at the Circle X Ranger Station.

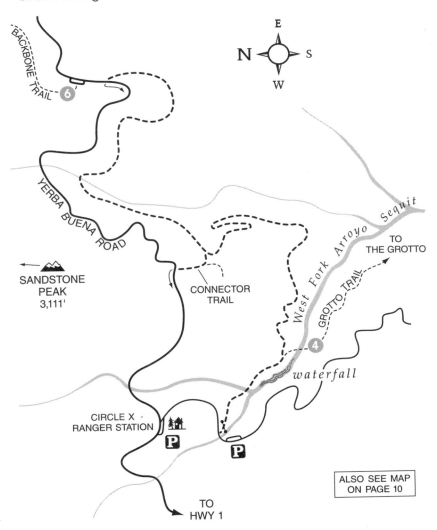

CANYON VIEW TRAIL–
YERBA BUENA ROAD
CIRCLE X RANCH

Hike 6
Mishe Mokwa—Backbone Loop
Sandstone Peak
CIRCLE X RANCH

Hiking distance: 6 mile loop
Hiking time: 3 hours
Elevation gain: 1,100 feet
Maps: U.S.G.S. Triunfo Pass and Newbury Park
      Santa Monica Mountains West Trail Map
      N.P.S. Circle X Ranch Site

Summary of hike: The Mishe Mokwa Trail in Circle X Ranch follows Carlisle Canyon along Boney Mountain past weathered red volcanic formations. There are views of the sculpted caves and crevices of Echo Cliffs and a forested streamside picnic area by a huge, split boulder known as Split Rock. The return route on the Backbone Trail leads to Inspiration Point and Sandstone Peak, the highest point in the Santa Monica Mountains. Both points overlook the Pacific Ocean, the Channel Islands, and the surrounding mountains.

Driving directions: Follow directions for Hike 4 to the Circle X Ranger Station. From the ranger station, continue one mile to the Backbone Trailhead parking lot on the left.

Hiking directions: Take the Backbone Trail (a fire road) uphill to the north. At 0.3 miles, leave the road and take the signed Mishe Mokwa Connector Trail straight ahead. Continue 0.2 miles to a junction with the Mishe Mokwa Trail and take the left fork. The trail contours along Boney Mountain on the western edge of Carlisle Canyon. At 1.4 miles, Balanced Rock can be seen on the opposite side of the canyon. Descend into the canyon shaded by oaks, laurel, and sycamores to Split Rock and the picnic area. Take the trail across the stream, heading out of the canyon to another stream crossing by sculptured volcanic rocks. Parallel the stream to a signed junction. Take the left fork—the Backbone Trail—curving uphill towards Inspiration

Point. A short side path leads up to the overlook. Continue east on the Backbone Trail to another junction. This side trail switchbacks up to the 360-degree views at Sandstone Peak. From the junction, it is 0.8 miles downhill back to the Mishe Mokwa junction, completing the loop.

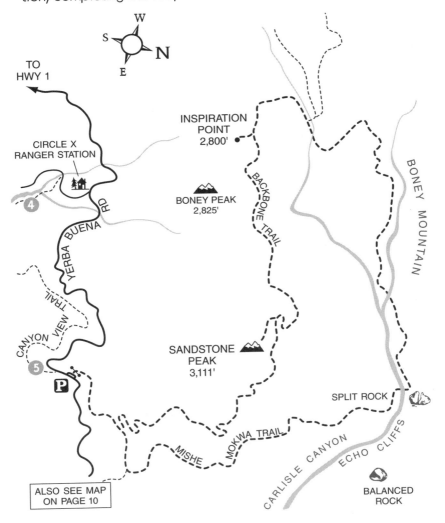

SANDSTONE PEAK LOOP
CIRCLE X RANCH

Hike 7
Big Sycamore Canyon Trail
POINT MUGU STATE PARK

Hiking distance: 8.4 miles one way (car shuttle)
Hiking time: 3 hours
Elevation loss: 900 feet
Maps: U.S.G.S. Newbury Park, Camarillo and Point Mugu
   Santa Monica Mountains West Trail Map
   N.P.S. Rancho Sierra Vista/Satwiwa map

Summary of hike: The Big Sycamore Canyon Trail is a one-way mountains-to the-sea journey. The trail, an unpaved service road, connects Newbury Park with the Sycamore Canyon Campground at the Pacific Ocean. The hike parallels Big Sycamore Creek through the heart of Point Mugu State Park in a deep, wooded canyon under towering sycamores and oaks.

Driving directions: For the shuttle car, follow the driving directions to Hike 3 and leave the car in the parking lot, where this hike ends.
   To the trailhead: From the shuttle car parking lot, drive 5.8 miles northbound on the Pacific Coast Highway/Highway 1 to Las Posas Road. Take Las Posas Road 2.9 miles north to Hueneme Road—turn right. Continue one mile to West Potrero Road and turn right. Drive 5.4 miles to Via Goleta and turn right (En route, West Potrero Road becomes Lynn Road). Drive 0.7 miles on Via Goleta to the parking lot at the end of the road.

Hiking directions: Take the posted trail past the restrooms a quarter mile to the service road at the Satwiwa Native American Indian Cultural Center. Bear right on the road, entering Point Mugu State Park, to a junction with the Boney Mountain Trail on the left. Begin the winding descent on the paved road to the canyon floor. The trail crosses a wooden bridge over the creek to the Hidden Pond Trail junction on the right. This is an excellent single track alternative trail that rejoins the Big Sycamore Canyon Trail 1.7 miles down canyon. On the alternative trail, there is a split at 2.2 miles. Take the left fork to the Sycamore Camping and Picnic Area. At 3 miles is a signed "beach" path on the right. This is where the alternative trail rejoins the service road. Just past the junction is the Danielson Ranch. Past the ranch, the trail is unpaved. Continue south down the forested canyon, past the Backbone Trail and the Overlook Trail (Hike 3) to the gate. From the gate, a paved road leads back to the shuttle car.

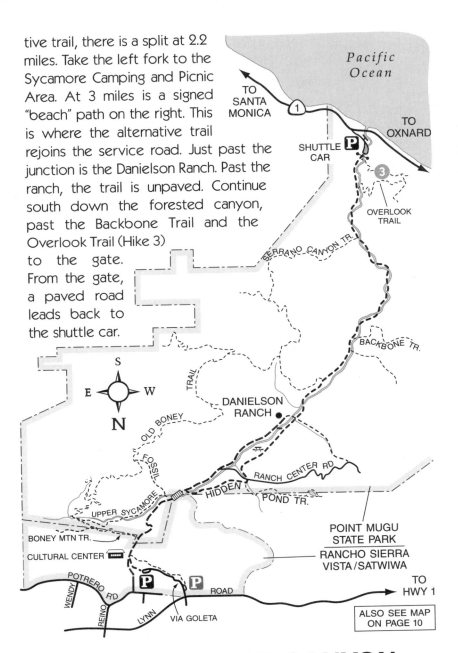

BIG SYCAMORE CANYON
POINT MUGU STATE PARK

Hike 8
White Horse Canyon Trail
LOS ROBLES TRAIL SYSTEM

Hiking distance: 3.5 mile loop
Hiking time: 1.5 hours

map
next page

Elevation gain: 500 feet
Maps: U.S.G.S. Thousand Oaks
Santa Monica Mountains West Trail Map
Los Robles Trail to Lake Sherwood map

Summary of hike: The Los Robles Trail System is a well-planned network of trails weaving through the growing residential communities of Westlake Village, Thousand Oaks, and Newbury Park. The multi-use trails link the open spaces of the inland valley with the oceanfront Santa Monica Mountains at Point Mugu State Park. This is an important wildlife corridor between the Santa Monica Mountains and the Simi Hills. The White Horse Canyon Trail, near the east end of the trail system, loops around the rolling, chaparral covered foothills to a ridge overlooking Westlake Village and Thousand Oaks. There is an additional overlook with a panoramic view of Lake Sherwood, the cliffs above Hidden Valley, and the Santa Monica Mountains.

Driving directions: From Ventura Freeway/Highway 101 in Thousand Oaks, exit on Westlake Boulevard. Drive 1.8 miles south to East Potrero Road and turn right. Continue 0.5 miles and park on the right across from the Foxfield Riding Club, just beyond the bridge over Potrero Valley Creek.

Hiking directions: From the parking area, the trailhead and kiosk are across the creekbed to the north. Head up the hill, past the homes on the right, to a fire road. The fire road leads to a junction. The left fork is a short side trip to a scenic overlook of Lake Sherwood. Back at the junction, take the north fork 0.5 miles to another junction with the White Horse Canyon Trail on the left. This footpath loops around the back side of the canyon before rejoining the fire road. Take the road to the right uphill a short distance to a junction with the Conejo Crest Trail on the left. Head left along the ridge as it descends back down to Potrero Valley Creek. Cross the creekbed into the park. Take the park path to the right, leading back to the parking area.

Hike 9
Triunfo Canyon Trail
LOS ROBLES TRAIL SYSTEM

Hiking distance: 2.5 mile loop
Hiking time: 1 hour
Elevation gain: 400 feet
Maps: U.S.G.S. Thousand Oaks
　　　Santa Monica Mountains West Trail Map
　　　Los Robles Trail to Lake Sherwood map

map
next page

Summary of hike: The Los Robles Trail System is a network of paths linking the Conejo and Russell Valleys by Westlake Village, Thousand Oaks, and Newbury Park with the Santa Monica Mountains at Point Mugu State Park. The multi-use trails connect numerous open spaces, thoughtfully blended with the encroaching residential areas. The Triunfo Canyon Trail is part of an open space near Westlake Village. The hike follows Triunfo Canyon to rolling grasslands on the ridge, where it connects with the Los Robles Trail. Atop the ridge are sweeping vistas of Westlake Village, the Conejo Valley, Lake Sherwood, and the Santa Monica Mountains.

Driving directions: From Ventura Freeway/Highway 101 in Thousand Oaks, exit on Hampshire Road. Drive 0.6 miles south to Triunfo Canyon Road and turn right. Continue 0.5 miles to Tamarack Street and turn right. The trailhead is 0.2 miles ahead in the parking lot at the north end of Triunfo Community Park.

Hiking directions: From the parking lot, head northwest on the signed trail past the kiosk. The trail gradually climbs along the contours of Triunfo Canyon to the ridgeline. Near the top, a short series of steep switchbacks lead to a bench. From the bench are great views of the valley below. The trail then levels out to a junction with the Los Robles Trail—go to the left. Thirty feet ahead is a ridge with views of the mountains and another

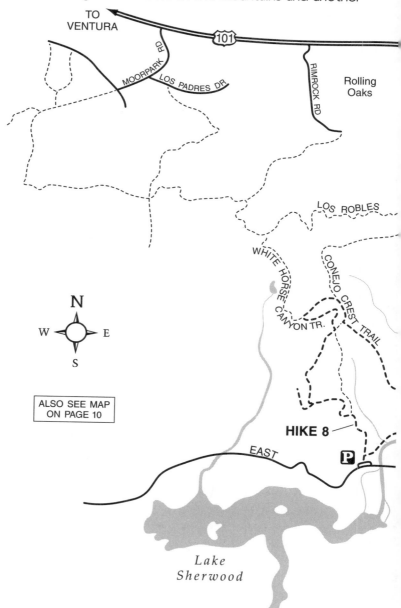

junction. Take the signed Los Robles Trail South to the left to a third trail split. Proceed downhill on the left fork. The trail ends at Brookview Avenue. Walk through the neighborhood one block to Stonesgate Street. Go to the left and proceed one block to Aranmoor Avenue. Go left again, returning to the park. The park path heads left, leading back to the parking lot.

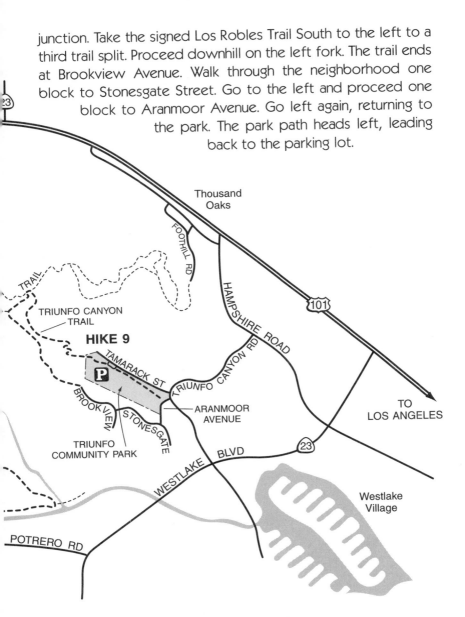

HIKES 8–9
WHITE HORSE CANYON
TRIUNFO CANYON

Hike 10
Lower Arroyo Sequit Trail and Sequit Point
LEO CARRILLO STATE BEACH

Hiking distance: 3 miles round trip
Hiking time: 1.5 hours
Elevation gain: 200 feet
Maps: U.S.G.S. Triunfo Pass
        Leo Carrillo State Beach map

Summary of hike: Leo Carrillo State Beach is a 2,000-acre haven with a 1.5-mile stretch of coastline, mountain canyons, and steep chaparral covered hillsides. The area was once inhabited by the Chumash Indians. The Lower Arroyo Sequit Trail leads into a cool, stream-fed canyon shaded with willow, sycamore, oak, and bay trees. The path ends in the deep-walled canyon by large multicolored boulders and the trickling stream. At the oceanfront, Sequit Point, a rocky bluff, juts out from the shoreline, dividing North Beach from South Beach. The weather-carved point has sea caves and coves, ocean-sculpted arches, tidepools, and pocket beaches.

Driving directions: From Santa Monica, drive 26 miles northbound on the Pacific Coast Highway/Highway 1 to the posted Leo Carrillo State Beach entrance and turn right. (The state park is 14 miles past Malibu Canyon Road.) Park in the day-use parking lot. A parking fee is required.

Hiking directions: Hike north through the campground on the road past mature sycamores and oaks. Pass the amphitheater on the right to a gated road. Continue past the gate, crossing over the seasonal Arroyo Sequit to the end of the paved road. Take the footpath a hundred yards, and rock hop over the creek by a small grotto. Follow the path upstream along the east side of the creek. Recross the creek to the trail's end in a steep-walled box canyon with pools and large boulders. Retrace your steps to the amphitheater, and now bear left on the footpath. Cross to the east side of the creek and head through the forest canopy. Switchbacks and two sets of wooden steps lead to a flat above the canyon. Descend back to the campground road.

To reach Sequit Point, take the paved path under Highway 1 to the sandy beach. To the right (west), by the lifeguard station, are sandstone rock formations with caves, tunnels, a rock arch, tidepools, and a series of beach coves.

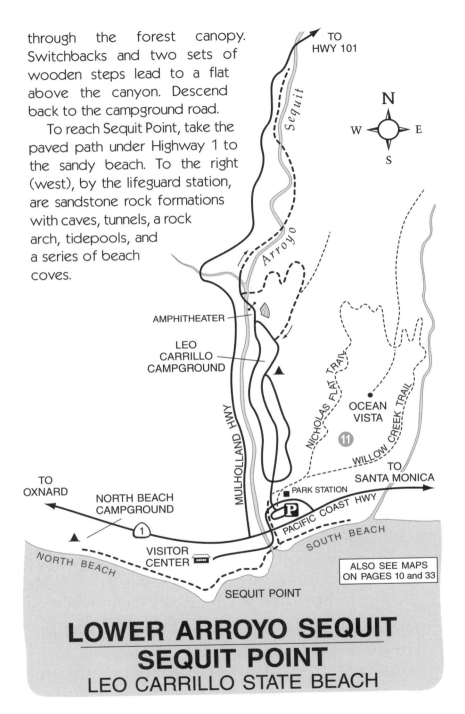

TO HWY 101

N
W ← → E
S

Sequit

Arroyo

AMPHITHEATER

LEO CARRILLO CAMPGROUND

NICHOLAS FLAT TRAIL

OCEAN VISTA

WILLOW CREEK TRAIL

MULHOLLAND HWY

11

TO SANTA MONICA

TO OXNARD

NORTH BEACH CAMPGROUND

1

PARK STATION

P

PACIFIC COAST HWY

SOUTH BEACH

VISITOR CENTER

NORTH BEACH

SEQUIT POINT

ALSO SEE MAPS ON PAGES 10 and 33

LOWER ARROYO SEQUIT
SEQUIT POINT
LEO CARRILLO STATE BEACH

Hike 11
Nicholas Flat and Willow Creek Loop
LEO CARRILLO STATE BEACH

Hiking distance: 2.5 mile loop
Hiking time: 1.3 hours
Elevation gain: 612 feet
Maps: U.S.G.S. Triunfo Pass
       Santa Monica Mountains West Trail Map
       Leo Carrillo State Beach map

Summary of hike: This loop hike in Leo Carrillo State Beach leads to Ocean Vista, a 612-foot bald knoll with great views of the Malibu coastline and Point Dume. The Willow Creek Trail traverses the east-facing hillside up Willow Creek Canyon to Ocean Vista. The hike returns along the Nicholas Flat Trail, one of the few trails connecting the Santa Monica Mountains to the Pacific Ocean.

Driving directions: From Santa Monica, drive 26 miles northbound on the Pacific Coast Highway/Highway 1 to the posted Leo Carrillo State Beach entrance and turn right. (The state park is 14 miles past Malibu Canyon Road.) Park in the day-use parking lot. A parking fee is required.

Hiking directions: The trailhead is 50 yards outside the park entrance station. Take the signed trail 100 yards northeast to a trail split. The loop begins at this junction. Take the right fork—the Willow Creek Trail—up the hillside and parallel to the ocean, heading east. At a half mile the trail curves north, traversing the hillside while overlooking the arroyo and Willow Creek. Three switchbacks lead aggressively up to a saddle and a signed four-way junction with the Nicholas Flat Trail. The left fork leads a quarter mile to Ocean Vista. After marveling at the views, return to the four-way junction and take the left (west) fork. Head downhill on the Nicholas Flat Trail across the grassy slopes above the park campground. Return to the junction near the trailhead.

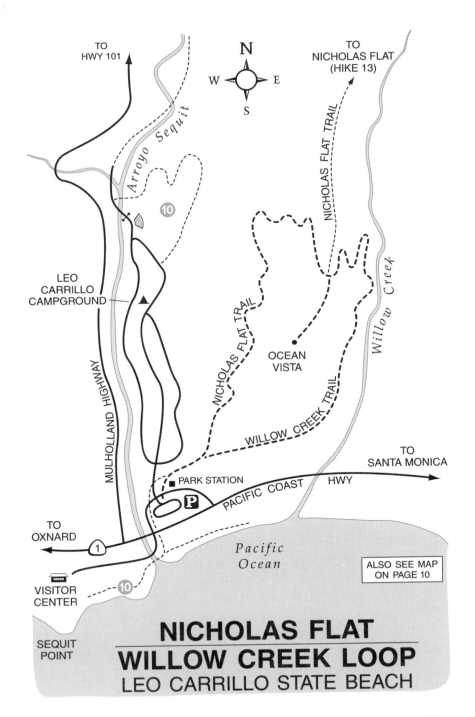

TO
HWY 101

N

W   E

S

Arroyo Sequit

⑩

LEO
CARRILLO
CAMPGROUND

▲

MULHOLLAND HIGHWAY

NICHOLAS FLAT TRAIL

OCEAN
VISTA

TO
NICHOLAS FLAT
(HIKE 13)

NICHOLAS FLAT TRAIL

Willow Creek

WILLOW CREEK TRAIL

TO
SANTA MONICA

■ PARK STATION

P

PACIFIC COAST HWY

TO
OXNARD

①

*Pacific
Ocean*

ALSO SEE MAP
ON PAGE 10

VISITOR
CENTER

⑩

SEQUIT
POINT

NICHOLAS FLAT
WILLOW CREEK LOOP
LEO CARRILLO STATE BEACH

Hike 12
Arroyo Sequit Park

Hiking distance: 2 mile loop
Hiking time: 1 hour
Elevation gain: 250 feet
Maps: U.S.G.S. Triunfo Pass
Santa Monica Mountains West Trail Map

Summary of hike: Arroyo Sequit Park was a ranch purchased by the Santa Monica Mountains Conservancy in 1985. Within the 155-acre park boundary are open grassland meadows, picnic areas, and a small canyon cut by the East Fork Arroyo Sequit with oak groves and a waterfall. From the meadows are panoramic views of the ocean and surrounding mountains. This easy loop hike visits the diverse park habitats, crossing the meadows and dropping into the gorge that runs parallel to the East Fork Arroyo Sequit.

Driving directions: From Santa Monica, drive 26.2 miles northbound on the Pacific Coast Highway/Highway 1 to Mulholland Highway and turn right. (Mulholland Highway is 14.2 miles past Malibu Canyon Road.) Continue 5.5 miles up the canyon to the signed turnoff on the right at mailbox 34138. Turn right into the park entrance and park.

Hiking directions: Head south on the park road past the gate, kiosk, and old ranch house. At 0.2 miles take the road to the left—past a barn, the astronomical observing site and picnic area—to the footpath on the right. Leave the service road on the nature trail, heading south. The trail skirts the east edge of the meadow, then descends into a small canyon and crosses several seasonal tributaries of the Arroyo Sequit. Head west along the southern wall of the canyon, passing a waterfall on the left. Cross a wooden footbridge over the stream, and descend to the canyon floor. Continue west, cross the East Fork Arroyo Sequit, and begin the ascent out of the canyon to a junction. Continue straight ahead up the hill. A series of switchbacks lead up the short but steep hill. Once at the top, cross the meadow to the road. Take the service road back to the parking area.

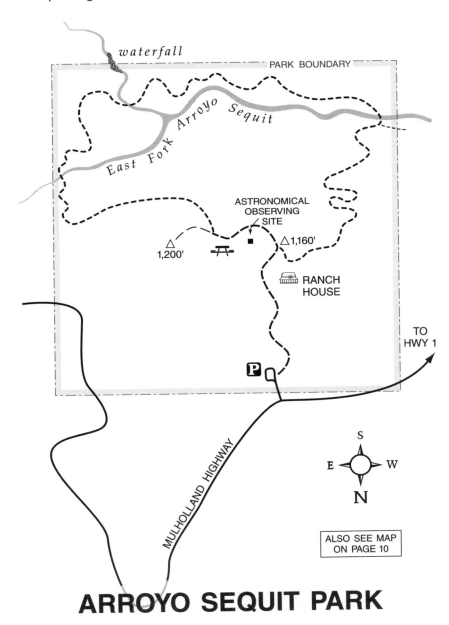

waterfall

PARK BOUNDARY

East Fork Arroyo Sequit

ASTRONOMICAL
OBSERVING
SITE

△
1,200'

△1,160'

RANCH
HOUSE

TO
HWY 1

P

MULHOLLAND HIGHWAY

S

E ✦ W

N

ALSO SEE MAP
ON PAGE 10

ARROYO SEQUIT PARK

Hike 13
Nicholas Flat
LEO CARRILLO STATE BEACH

Hiking distance: 2.5 mile double loop
Hiking time: 1.3 hours
Elevation gain: 100 feet
Maps: U.S.G.S. Triunfo Pass
  Santa Monica Mountains West Trail Map
  Leo Carrillo State Beach map

Summary of hike: Nicholas Flat, in the upper reaches of Leo Carrillo State Beach, is a grassy highland meadow with large oak trees, an old cattle pond, and sandstone outcroppings 1,700 feet above the sea. This hike skirts around Nicholas Flat with spectacular views of the ocean, San Nicholas Canyon, and the surrounding mountains. The Nicholas Flat Trail may be hiked 3.5 miles downhill to the Pacific Ocean, connecting to Hike 11.

Driving directions: From Santa Monica, drive 23.8 miles northbound on the Pacific Coast Highway/Highway 1 to Decker Road and turn right. (Decker Road is 11.8 miles past Malibu Canyon Road.) Continue 2.4 miles north to Decker School Road and turn left. Drive 1.5 miles to the road's end and park alongside the road.

Hiking directions: Hike south past the gate and kiosk. Stay on the wide, oak-lined trail to a junction at 0.3 miles. Take the right fork, beginning the first loop. At 0.6 miles is another junction. Again take the right fork—the Meadows Trail. Continue past the Malibu Springs Trail on the right to Vista Point, where there are great views into the canyons. The trail curves south to a junction with the Nicholas Flat Trail, leading to Leo Carrillo State Beach. Take the left fork around the perimeter of the flat. A trail on the right leads to another vista point. Complete the first loop at 1.8 miles. Take the trail to the right at two successive junctions to a pond. Follow along the pond through the meadow, completing the second loop. Return to the trailhead.

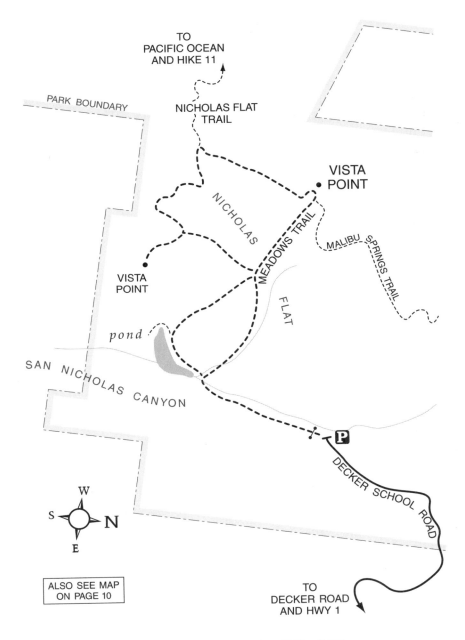

TO
PACIFIC OCEAN
AND HIKE 11

PARK BOUNDARY

NICHOLAS FLAT
TRAIL

VISTA
POINT

NICHOLAS

MEADOWS TRAIL

MALIBU SPRINGS TRAIL

VISTA
POINT

FLAT

pond

SAN NICHOLAS CANYON

P

DECKER SCHOOL ROAD

W
S — N
E

ALSO SEE MAP
ON PAGE 10

TO
DECKER ROAD
AND HWY 1

NICHOLAS FLAT
LEO CARRILLO STATE BEACH

Hike 14
Charmlee County Park
Open 8:00 a.m. to sunset daily

Hiking distance: 3 mile loop
Hiking time: 1.5 hours
Elevation gain: 600 feet
Maps: U.S.G.S. Triunfo Pass
Santa Monica Mountains West Trail Map
City of Malibu—Charmlee Natural Area map

Summary of hike: Perched on oceanfront cliffs 1,300 feet above the sea, Charmlee County Park has a magnificent bird's-eye view of the Malibu coastline. The 460-acre wilderness park was an old cattle ranch, purchased by Los Angeles County in 1968 and opened as a county park in 1981. A network of interconnecting footpaths and old ranch roads weave through expansive grassy meadows, oak and eucalyptus woodlands, mountain slopes, rocky ridges, and 1,250-foot bluffs overlooking the sea. The park has picnic areas and a nature center with plant exhibits.

Driving directions: From Santa Monica, drive 23.2 miles northbound on the Pacific Coast Highway/Highway 1 to Encinal Canyon Road and turn right. (Encinal Canyon Road is 11.2 miles past Malibu Canyon Road.) Continue 3.7 miles to the park entrance on the left. Drive 0.2 miles on the park road to the parking lot.

Hiking directions: Hike past the information board and picnic area on the wide trail. Pass a second picnic area on the left in an oak grove, and continue uphill to a three-way trail split. The middle trail is a short detour leading to an overlook set among rock formations and an old house foundation. Take the main trail to the left into the large grassy meadow. Two trails cross the meadow and rejoin at the south end—the main trail heads through the meadow while the right fork skirts the meadow's western edge. At the far end is an ocean overlook and a trail fork. Bear left past an old ranch reservoir, and pass two junctions to a 1,200-foot overlook on the right. Continue downhill, curving north through an oak grove to the unsigned Botany Trail, a narrow footpath on the right. The Botany Trail winds back to the picnic area and the trailhead.

OVERLOOKS

reservoir

PARK BOUNDARY

LECHUSA CANYON

MEADOW

OVERLOOK

S
E — W
N

ALSO SEE MAP
ON PAGE 10

BOTANY TRAIL

NATURE
CENTER

P

ENCINAL CANYON ROAD

TO
HWY 1

CHARMLEE
COUNTY PARK

Hike 15
Zuma Loop Trail
ZUMA/TRANCAS CANYONS: Lower Zuma Canyon

Hiking distance: 1.7 mile loop
Hiking time: 1 hour
Elevation gain: 250 feet
Maps: U.S.G.S. Point Dume
        Santa Monica Mountains West Trail Map
        N.P.S. Zuma/Trancas Canyons map

Summary of hike: Zuma Canyon is one of the few canyons in the Santa Monica Mountains that is accessible only to foot and horse traffic. There are no paved roads. This hike begins on the Zuma Canyon Trail in Lower Zuma Canyon. The trail heads up the drainage parallel to Zuma Creek past lush riparian vegetation, oak, willow, and sycamore trees. The hike returns on the Zuma Loop Trail above the canyon floor, traversing the east-facing hillside overlooking the canyon and the ocean.

Driving directions: From Santa Monica, drive 21 miles northbound on the Pacific Coast Highway/Highway 1 to Bonsall Drive and turn right. (The turnoff is one mile past Kanan Dume Road.) Continue one mile north to the trailhead parking area at road's end. The last 200 yards are on an unpaved lane.

Hiking directions: From the end of the road, hike north past the trailhead gate on the Zuma Canyon Trail. At 0.2 miles is a junction with the Zuma Loop Trail. Go straight on the Zuma Canyon Trail past oak and sycamore trees. Continue past the junction with the Ocean View Trail on the right, cross Zuma Creek, and head to a junction with the Canyon View Trail. Bear left and remain close to the creek. At 0.7 miles, cross Zuma Creek to a junction. To add an additional 1.4 miles to the hike, take the right fork 0.7 miles up the canyon, crossing the creek several times to the trail's end. Return to the junction, and take the Zuma Loop Trail to the west, traversing the hillside. Follow the ridge south, bearing left at three separate trail forks before returning down to the canyon floor and completing the loop. Take the right fork back to the trailhead.

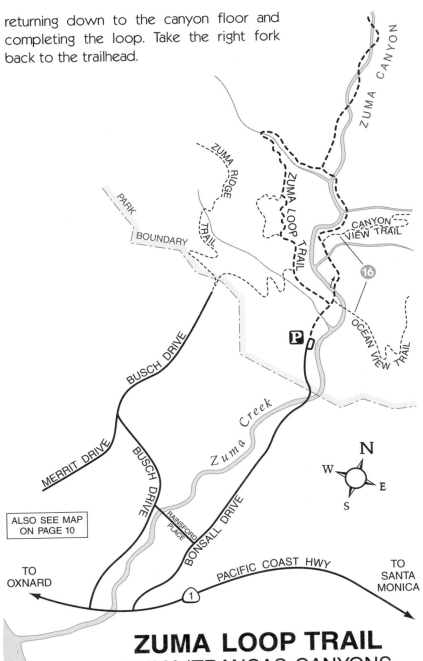

ZUMA LOOP TRAIL
ZUMA/TRANCAS CANYONS

Hike 16
Ocean View—Canyon View Loop
ZUMA/TRANCAS CANYONS: Lower Zuma Canyon

Hiking distance: 3.1 miles round trip
Hiking time: 1.5 hours
Elevation gain: 600 feet
Maps: U.S.G.S. Point Dume
Santa Monica Mountains West Trail Map
N.P.S. Zuma/Trancas Canyons map

Summary of hike: Zuma Canyon remains a beautiful, natural gorge with minimal development in Lower Zuma Canyon. The perennial stream makes its way down the canyon floor, reaching the ocean at the west end of Point Dume. From the parking area, a trail follows the canyon bottom and links to a network of hiking trails. This hike ascends the eastern hillside on the Ocean View Trail and returns back to the canyon on the Canyon View Trail. Throughout the hike are great views of Point Dume, the coastline, and upper Zuma Canyon.

Driving directions: Same as Hike 15.

Hiking directions: From the mouth of the canyon, head north up the canyon floor for 0.2 miles to a signed junction. The Zuma Canyon Loop (Hike 15) curves left. Stay on the canyon bottom 30 yards to the posted Ocean View Trail. Bear right, cross a rocky streambed, and ascend the east canyon wall. Wind up the hillside to views of Point Dume and the ocean, reaching the ridge at 1.3 miles. At the summit are sweeping coastal views that extend (on clear days) to Palos Verdes, Point Mugu, and Catalina. The Ocean View Trail ends at a T-junction, but the ocean views continue throughout the hike. Bear left 0.1 mile on the unpaved Kanan Edison Road to a junction with the Canyon View Trail. Curve left and follow the ridge across the head of the small side canyon. Weave down the hillside to the canyon floor and a junction at 2.6 miles. Bear left on the Zuma Canyon Trail and walk down canyon. Parallel the small stream past laurel sumac bushes and sycamore trees. Complete the loop and return to the trailhead.

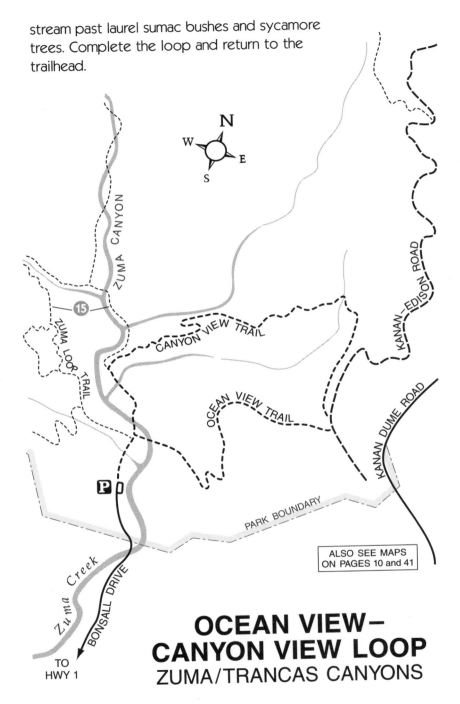

OCEAN VIEW–
CANYON VIEW LOOP
ZUMA/TRANCAS CANYONS

Hike 17
Newton Canyon Falls
ZUMA / TRANCAS CANYONS: Upper Zuma Canyon

Hiking distance: 1.5 miles round trip
Hiking time: 1 hour
Elevation gain: 200 feet
Maps: U.S.G.S. Point Dume
            Santa Monica Mountains West Trail Map

Summary of hike: The Upper Zuma Canyon Trail begins in Newton Canyon. The trail leads a short distance along a portion of the Backbone Trail to Newton Canyon Falls, a year-round, 30-foot waterfall in a lush, forested grotto with mossy rocks and a tangle of vines (cover photo). There are large, shaded boulders to sit on near the falls by cascading Newton Creek.

Driving directions: From Santa Monica, drive 18 miles northbound on the Pacific Coast Highway/Highway 1 to Kanan Dume Road (5.8 miles past Malibu Canyon Road). Turn right and drive 4.4 miles north to the trailhead parking lot on the left. The parking lot is located just after the first tunnel (T-1).
     From the Ventura Freeway/Highway 101 in Agoura Hills, exit on Kanan Road. Drive 7.9 miles south to the trailhead parking lot on the right. The parking lot is located just before entering the third tunnel (T-1). (Kanan Road becomes Kanan Dume Road after it crosses Mulholland Highway.)

Hiking directions: Hike west, away from Kanan Dume Road, on the signed Backbone Trail. The trail immediately begins its descent from the open chaparral into the shady canyon. After crossing the trickling Newton Creek, a side trail on the left leads 20 yards to sandstone rocks at the top of the falls. The main trail continues 100 yards downhill to a second cutoff trail on the left. Take this steep side path downhill through a forest of oaks, sycamores, and bay laurels to the creek, bearing to the left on the descent. Once at the creek, hike upstream along the path. Fifty yards up the narrow canyon is a lush grotto at the base of Newton Canyon Falls. The main trail continues west into the rugged Zuma Canyon with steep volcanic cliffs. After enjoying the waterfall, return by retracing your steps.

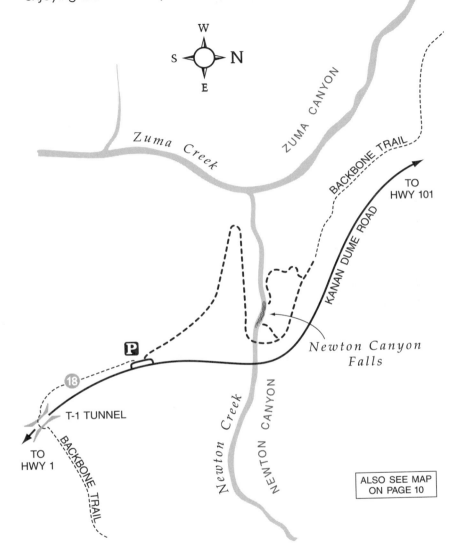

NEWTON CANYON FALLS
ZUMA/TRANCAS CANYONS

Hike 18
Newton Canyon
ZUMA / TRANCAS CANYONS

Hiking distance: 4.6 miles round trip
Hiking time: 2.5 hours
Elevation gain: 300 feet
Maps: U.S.G.S. Point Dume
Santa Monica Mountains West Trail Map

Summary of hike: This hike parallels Newton Canyon along a 2.3-mile portion of the Backbone Trail between Kanan Dume Road and Latigo Canyon Road. The forested trail winds along the south ridge of the dense oak-filled canyon with ocean views and seasonal stream crossings.

Driving directions: From Santa Monica, drive 18 miles northbound on the Pacific Coast Highway/Highway 1 to Kanan Dume Road (5.8 miles past Malibu Canyon Road). Turn right and drive 4.4 miles north to the trailhead parking lot on the left. The parking lot is located just after the first tunnel (T-1).

From the Ventura Freeway/Highway 101 in Agoura Hills, exit on Kanan Road. Drive 7.9 miles south to the trailhead parking lot on the right. The parking lot is located just before entering the third tunnel (T-1). (Kanan Road becomes Kanan Dume Road after it crosses Mulholland Highway.)

Hiking directions: The signed trail begins by Kanan Dume Road and heads south towards the ocean. The trail, an old fire road, climbs up to the tunnel and crosses over Kanan Dume Road. After crossing, the road narrows to a footpath and enters a forested canopy, slowly descending into the canyon. The trail crosses a paved driveway, then climbs to various overlooks. Continue along the winding mountainside above Newton Canyon. Near the end of the trail, a maze-like series of switchbacks lead to Latigo Canyon Road. This is the turnaround spot.

To hike further, cross the road to the trailhead parking area, and continue on the Backbone Trail. It is another 1.4 miles to

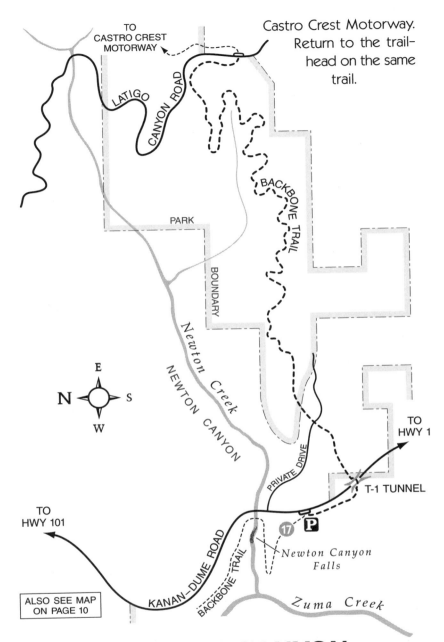

TO
CASTRO CREST
MOTORWAY

Castro Crest Motorway.
Return to the trail-
head on the same
trail.

LATIGO CANYON ROAD

BACKBONE TRAIL

PARK

BOUNDARY

Newton Creek

NEWTON CANYON

E

N ⊕ S

W

PRIVATE DRIVE

TO
HWY 1

T-1 TUNNEL

TO
HWY 101

KANAN–DUME ROAD

BACKBONE TRAIL

⑰ P

*Newton Canyon
Falls*

ALSO SEE MAP
ON PAGE 10

Zuma Creek

NEWTON CANYON
ZUMA/TRANCAS CANYONS

Hike 19
Rocky Oaks Park

Hiking distance: 2 mile loop
Hiking time: 1 hour
Elevation gain: 200 feet
Maps: U.S.G.S. Point Dume
Santa Monica Mountains West Trail Map
N.P.S. Rocky Oaks Site

Summary of hike: Rocky Oaks Park was once a working cattle ranch resting at the head of Zuma Canyon. The pastoral 200-acre ranch was purchased by the National Park Service in 1981. The park includes oak savannahs, rolling grasslands, chaparral covered hills, volcanic rock formations, scenic overlooks, picnic areas, and a pond in the grassy meadow. This easy loop hike meanders through the park, visiting each of these diverse ecological communities.

Driving directions: From Santa Monica, drive 18 miles northbound on the Pacific Coast Highway/Highway 1 to Kanan Dume Road (5.8 miles past Malibu Canyon Road). Turn right and drive 6.2 miles north to Mulholland Highway and turn left. Quickly turn right into the Rocky Oaks Park entrance and parking lot.

From the Ventura Freeway/Highway 101 in Agoura Hills, exit on Kanan Road. Drive 6.1 miles south to Mulholland Highway. Turn right and a quick right again into the park entrance.

Hiking directions: Hike north past the rail fence to the Rocky Oaks Loop Trail, which heads in both directions. Take the left fork a short distance to a 4-way junction. Continue straight ahead on the middle path towards the Overlook Trail. Ascend the hillside overlooking the pond, and take the horseshoe bend to the left. Beyond the bend is the Overlook Trail. This is a short detour on the left to a scenic overlook with panoramic views. Back on the main trail, continue northeast around the ridge, slowly descending to the valley floor near Kanan Road. Bear sharply to the right, heading south to the Pond Trail junction. Both the left and right forks loop around the pond and rejoin at the south end. At the junction, go south and back to the Rocky Oaks Loop, then retrace your steps back to the trailhead.

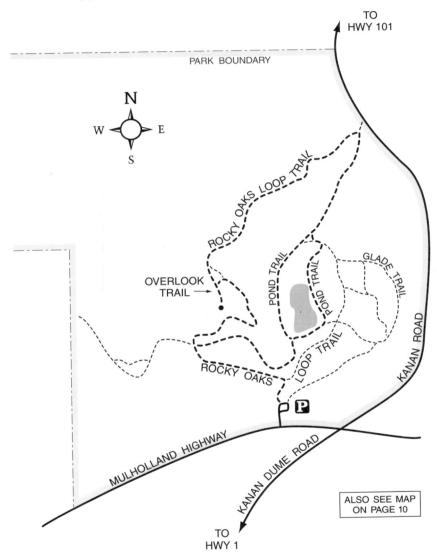

ROCKY OAKS PARK

Hike 20
China Flat Trail
CHEESEBORO/PALO COMADO CANYONS

Hiking distance: 4 mile loop
Hiking time: 2 hours
Elevation gain: 1,000 feet
Maps: U.S.G.S. Thousand Oaks
   N.P.S. Cheeseboro/Palo Comado Canyons

Summary of hike: China Flat, a newer addition to the Cheeseboro/Palo Comado Canyons site, is a high, oak-dotted grassland meadow with sedimentary rock outcroppings. The flat is perched on the west side of Palo Comado Canyon beneath the shadows of Simi Peak, the highest peak in the Simi Hills. The China Flat Trail is a steep hike with awesome, panoramic views of Simi Valley, Oak Park, Agoura Hills, and Westlake Village. Connector trails link China Flat to the upper reaches of Palo Comado and Cheeseboro Canyons (Hikes 21 and 22).

Driving directions: From Ventura Freeway/Highway 101 in Westlake Village, exit on Lindero Canyon Road. Drive 4 miles north and park on Lindero Canyon Road by the China Flat Trailhead on the left. It is located between King James Court and Wembly Avenue.

Hiking directions: Hike north past the trailhead sign towards the mountains. Climb the short, steep hill to where a trail from King James Court merges with the main trail. Continue around the east side of a large sandstone outcropping. The trail levels out and heads east, following the contour of the mountain base, to an unsigned junction. Take the left fork north, heading uphill towards the ridge. Once over the ridge, the trail meets another unsigned junction. Take the left fork and head west, with views overlooking the canyon. Proceed uphill along the ridgeline to a flat area and trail junction. The right fork leads back towards Palo Comado and Cheeseboro Canyons. Take the left fork and descend to another junction. Again, take the left fork, winding downhill to a gate at King James Court. Leave the trail and walk one block on the sidewalk to Lindero Canyon Road. The trailhead is on the left.

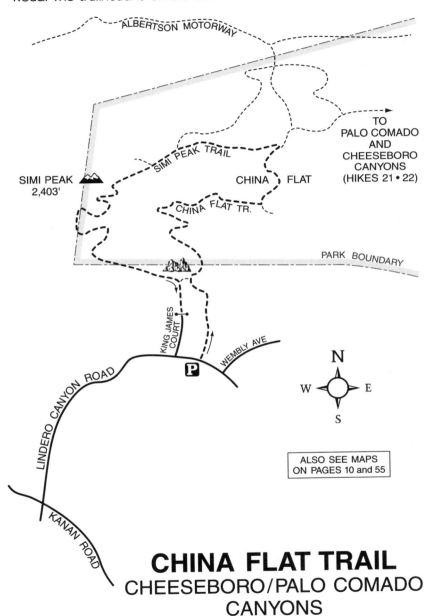

CHINA FLAT TRAIL
CHEESEBORO/PALO COMADO CANYONS

Hike 21
Palo Comado—Cheeseboro Canyons Loop
CHEESEBORO/PALO COMADO CANYONS

Hiking distance: 5 mile loop
Hiking time: 2.5 hours
Elevation gain: 800 feet
Maps: U.S.G.S. Thousand Oaks and Calabasas
N.P.S. Cheeseboro/Palo Comado Canyons

Summary of hike: Palo Comado and Cheeseboro Canyons, in the Simi Hills near Agoura Hills, is a wildlife corridor connecting the Santa Monica Mountains with the Santa Susana Mountains. This north–south corridor allows animals to move freely between the two ranges. This loop hike heads up the undeveloped Palo Comado Canyon parallel to a stream and meadows. After crossing over into Cheeseboro Canyon, the hike follows the canyon floor on an old ranch road through grasslands with groves of stately valley oaks and twisted coast live oaks.

Driving directions: From Ventura Freeway/Highway 101 in Agoura Hills, exit on Kanan Road. Head north 2.2 miles to Sunnycrest Drive and turn right. Continue 0.8 miles to the "Public Open Space" sign on the right. Park along the curb.

Hiking directions: From the trailhead, hike east past the gate and up a short hill on the Sunnycrest Connector Trail. As you top the hill, the trail descends into Palo Comado Canyon. Cross the stream at the canyon floor to a junction with the Palo Comado Canyon Trail, an old ranch road. Head left up the canyon through rolling grasslands with sycamore and oak groves. At one mile the trail begins to climb out of the canyon, winding along the contours of the mountain. Near the head of the canyon, the Palo Comado Canyon Trail curves left, heading to China Flat (Hike 20). There is an unmarked but distinct path leading sharply to the right at the beginning of this curve—the Old Sheep Corral Trail. Take this path uphill to a couple of ridges that overlook Cheeseboro Canyon. Descend into the canyon a short distance to the corral and a junction at Shepherds' Flat. Straight ahead the trail climbs up to Cheeseboro Ridge. Take the right fork and follow Cheeseboro Canyon gently downhill. At Sulphur Springs, identified by its smell, walk beneath the white sedimentary cliffs of the Baleen Wall on the east canyon wall. Continue down canyon through oak groves to the posted Ranch Center Connector Trail, 1.3 miles down the canyon on the right. Bear right and wind 1.1 mile up and over the chaparral hillside from Cheeseboro Canyon back to Palo Comado Canyon. Bear right a short distance, completing the loop. Return to the left on the Sunnycrest Connector Trail.

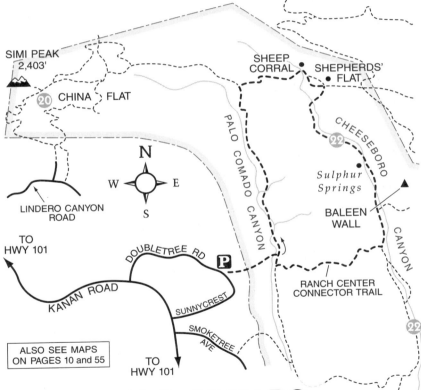

PALO COMADO–
CHEESEBORO CANYONS
LOOP

Hike 22
Cheeseboro Canyon to Shepherds' Flat
CHEESEBORO/PALO COMADO CANYONS

Hiking distance: 8.6 miles round trip
Hiking time: 4 hours
Elevation gain: 600 feet
Maps: U.S.G.S. Calabasas
      N.P.S. Cheeseboro/Palo Comado Canyons

Summary of hike: Cheeseboro Canyon is a lush stream-fed canyon with large valley oaks, gnarled coast live oaks, and sycamores. The hike follows an old abandoned ranch road on a gentle grade up the forested canyon bottom. The trail passes fragrant Sulphur Springs as you pass beneath the Baleen Wall, a vertical rock formation on the east canyon wall. At the upper reaches of the canyon is Shepherds' Flat, a grassland flat and a sheep corral.

Driving directions: From Ventura Freeway/Highway 101 in Agoura Hills, exit on Chesebro Road. Continue one block straight ahead, past the stop sign, to Palo Comado Canyon Road and turn left. Drive 0.3 miles to Chesebro Road again and turn right. Continue 0.7 miles to Cheeseboro Canyon Road and turn right. The trailhead parking lot is 0.2 miles ahead.

Hiking directions: Take the service road east toward Cheeseboro Canyon to a road split. Bear left on the Cheeseboro Canyon Trail, heading into the canyon past the Modelo Trail and the Canyon View Trail. At 1.3 miles is a junction with the Cheeseboro Ridge Connector Trail (also known as the Baleen Wall Trail). Take the left fork towards Sulphur Springs to another junction with the Modelo Trail on the left. Proceed a short distance on the main trail to a junction. Take the left branch. As you near Sulphur Springs, the white, jagged cliffs of the Baleen Wall can be seen towering on the cliffs to the east. At 3.5 miles, the canyon and trail both narrow as the smell of sulphur becomes stronger. At the head of the canyon is a three-way junction at Shepherds' Flat, the turnaround point. Return back to the Modelo Trail junction. Take the Modelo Trail along the western ridge of the canyon back to the trailhead.

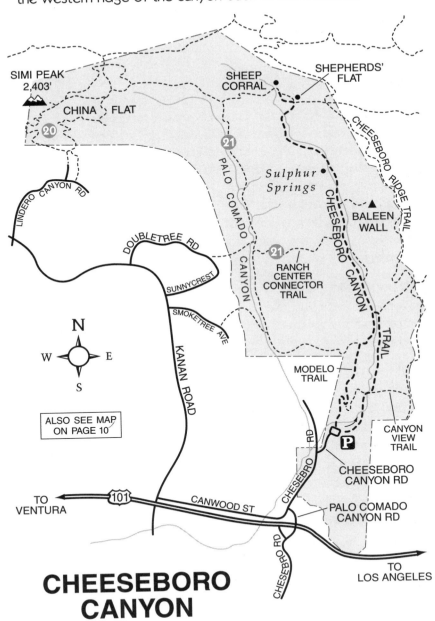

CHEESEBORO CANYON

Hike 23
Chumash Trail
ROCKY PEAK PARK

Hiking distance: 5 miles round trip
Hiking time: 2.5 hours
Elevation gain: 1,100 feet
Maps: U.S.G.S. Simi Valley East

Summary of hike: The Chumash Trail ascends the west flank of Rocky Peak in the Santa Susana Mountains east of Simi Valley. The trail winds up the chaparral cloaked mountainside to the ridge north of Rocky Peak, passing sculpted sandstone out-croppings, caves, and a series of scenic overlooks and highland meadows. From Hamilton Saddle and the Rocky Peak Trail junction are panoramic views of the Simi Hills, Simi Valley, San Fernando Valley, the Santa Susana Mountains, the Santa Monica Mountains, Blind Canyon, and Las Llajas Canyon.

Driving directions: From Highway 118/Ronald Reagan Freeway in Simi Valley, exit on Yosemite Avenue. Drive 0.4 miles north to Flanagan Drive and turn right. Continue 0.8 miles to the trailhead at the end of the road.

Hiking directions: Head north past the kiosk along the rolling hills and grassy meadows. The trail climbs steadily as you round the hillside to the first overlook of the Simi Hills to the south. The trail continues uphill through coastal sage scrub, curving left around the next rolling hill. The trail passes sculpted sandstone formations. Arrow signposts are placed along the route. Continue to the east along the edge of the canyon to Hamilton Saddle. From the saddle, the trail sharply curves left (north), gaining elevation before leveling out again at Flat Rock. From Flat Rock, the trail begins its final ascent through chapar-ral, curving around the last ridge to the top. The trail ends at a junction with the Rocky Peak Trail at an elevation of 2,450 feet. Sixty yards to the left of the junction are views of Blind Canyon and Las Llajas Canyon. Reverse your route to return.

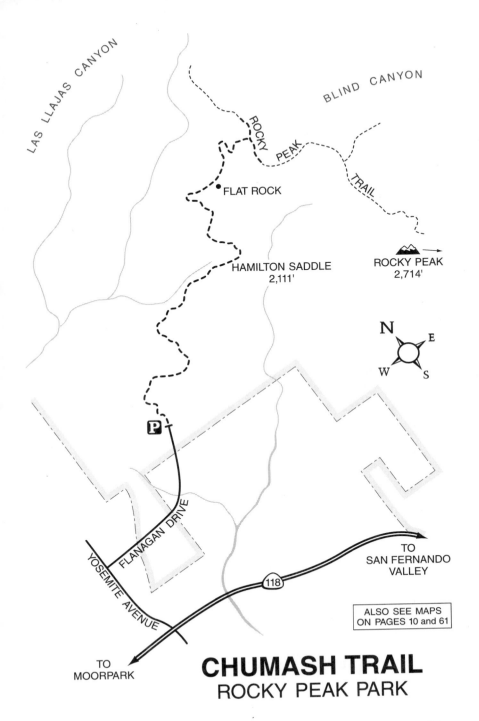

LAS LLAJAS CANYON

BLIND CANYON

ROCKY PEAK TRAIL

● FLAT ROCK

HAMILTON SADDLE
2,111'

ROCKY PEAK
2,714'

N
E
W
S

P

FLANAGAN DRIVE

YOSEMITE AVENUE

118

TO
SAN FERNANDO
VALLEY

TO
MOORPARK

ALSO SEE MAPS
ON PAGES 10 and 61

CHUMASH TRAIL
ROCKY PEAK PARK

Hike 24
Hummingbird Trail
ROCKY PEAK PARK

Hiking distance: 4.6 miles round trip
Hiking time: 2 hours
Elevation gain: 1,000 feet
Maps: U.S.G.S. Simi Valley East

Summary of hike: Rocky Peak Park in the Santa Susana Mountains straddles the Los Angeles-Ventura county line at the eastern end of Simi Valley. A network of hiking trails weaves through the 4,815-acre park that is home to deep oak-lined canyons, trickling streams, and massive, sculpted sandstone formations with a moonscape appearance. The Hummingbird Trail, at the base of Rocky Peak, crosses Hummingbird Creek and climbs up a narrow canyon through open chaparral to the Rocky Peak Fire Road, passing stacks of giant sandstone boulders, sculpted caves, and dramatic rock outcroppings.

Driving directions: From Highway 118/Ronald Reagan Freeway in Simi Valley, exit on Kuehner Drive. Drive 0.3 miles north to the signed trailhead on the right. Park in one of the pull-outs alongside the road. If full, additional parking is available just north of the freeway.

Hiking directions: From the trailhead kiosk, head downhill to the north. The trail soon U-turns southeast into the canyon to a defunct rock dam from 1917 and Hummingbird Creek. Proceed past the dam into an oak woodland and meadow. Once past the meadow, the trail crosses Hummingbird Creek and begins the ascent up the mountain through chaparral. Switchbacks lead up to sandstone caves and rock formations. After the rocks and caves, the trail levels out before the second ascent. Switchbacks make the climb easier as it heads up the canyon. At the head of the canyon, the trail levels out and passes more rock formations. The trail ends at a junction with the Rocky Peak Trail—Hike 25. Return to the trailhead by retracing your steps.

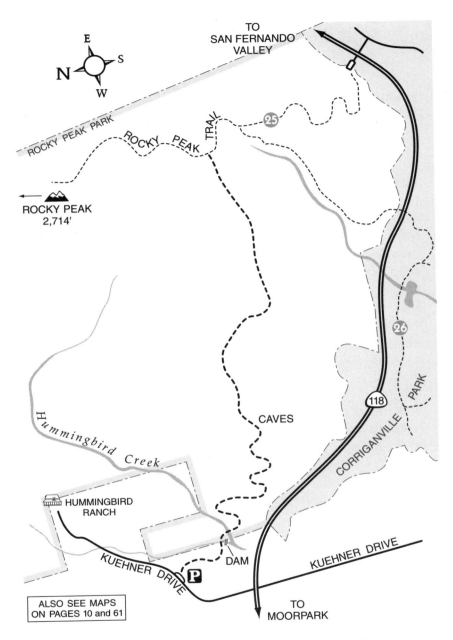

TO
SAN FERNANDO
VALLEY

E
N ⊕ S
W

ROCKY PEAK PARK

ROCKY PEAK TRAIL

25

ROCKY PEAK
2,714'

26

118

CAVES

CORRIGANVILLE PARK

Hummingbird Creek

HUMMINGBIRD
RANCH

KUEHNER DRIVE

DAM

KUEHNER DRIVE

P

TO
MOORPARK

ALSO SEE MAPS
ON PAGES 10 and 61

HUMMINGBIRD TRAIL
ROCKY PEAK PARK

Hike 25
Rocky Peak Trail
ROCKY PEAK PARK

Hiking distance: 5–6 miles round trip
Hiking time: 2.5 hours
Elevation gain: 1,100 feet
Maps: U.S.G.S. Simi Valley East

Summary of hike: Rocky Peak Park is aptly named for the dramatic sandstone formations, fractured boulders, overhangs, and outcroppings. The 4,815-acre wilderness park is located in Simi Valley by Santa Susana Pass. The park is a critical wildlife habitat linkage between the Simi Hills and the Santa Susana Mountains. Rocky Peak Trail follows a winding fire road on the north side of the 118 freeway to Rocky Peak, which lies on the Los Angeles-Ventura county line. There are a series of vista points along the route and at the jagged 2,714-foot peak, including top-of-the-world views of the San Fernando Valley, Simi Valley, the Santa Monica Mountains, and the many peaks of the Los Padres National Forest.

Driving directions: From Highway 118/Ronald Reagan Freeway in Simi Valley, exit on Kuehner Drive. Drive 3 miles south to the Highway 118 East on-ramp. (Along the way, Kuehner Drive becomes Santa Susana Pass Road.) Turn left, crossing over the freeway, and park 0.1 mile ahead at the end of the road.

Hiking directions: Hike past the trailhead kiosk up the winding fire road to an unsigned trail split at 0.9 miles. Stay to the left on the main trail, hiking steadily uphill to a signed junction with the Hummingbird Trail on the left (Hike 24). Proceed straight ahead on the Rocky Peak Trail, which levels out. The winding trail offers alternating views of the San Fernando Valley to the east and Simi Valley to the west. At the base of the final ascent is a singular, large oak tree. Begin the steep ascent, gaining 450 feet in a half mile, to the Rocky Peak Cutoff Trail. This is a good turnaround spot.

However, if you wish to hike to the summit, the trail takes off to the right across the plateau for a half mile to Rocky Peak. The last portion is a rock scramble to the peak. To return, reverse your route.

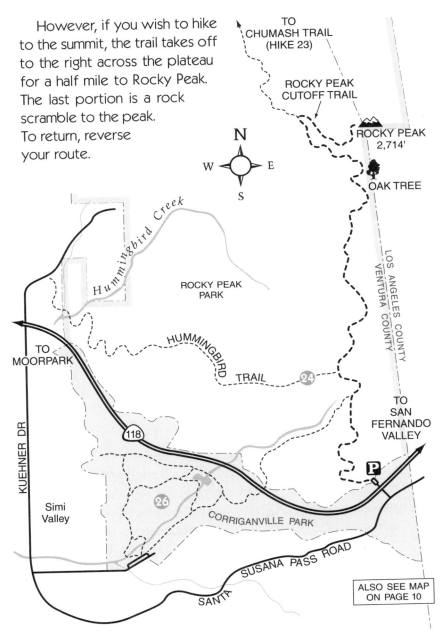

TO
CHUMASH TRAIL
(HIKE 23)

ROCKY PEAK
CUTOFF TRAIL

ROCKY PEAK
2,714'

OAK TREE

N

W   E

S

Hummingbird Creek

ROCKY PEAK
PARK

LOS ANGELES COUNTY
VENTURA COUNTY

TO
MOORPARK

HUMMINGBIRD
TRAIL   24

118

KUEHNER DR

TO
SAN
FERNANDO
VALLEY

P

Simi
Valley

26

CORRIGANVILLE PARK

SANTA SUSANA PASS ROAD

ALSO SEE MAP
ON PAGE 10

ROCKY PEAK TRAIL
ROCKY PEAK PARK

Hike 26
Corriganville Park

Hiking distance: 2 miles round trip
Hiking time: 1 hour
Elevation gain: 100 feet
Maps: U.S.G.S. Simi Valley East
       Rancho Simi Open Space: Corriganville Park

Summary of hike: Corriganville Park, at the eastern end of Simi Valley, was an old movie ranch. It was the setting to about a thousand movie and television shows between 1937 and 1965, including *The Lone Ranger, Gunsmoke, The Fugitive, Lassie, Mutiny on the Bounty, African Queen, How The West Was Won,* and *Fort Apache*, to name just a few. Old stone and concrete foundations from the sets still remain. The oak-shaded paths lead through the 225-acre park past prominent sandstone outcroppings, cliffs, caves, a stream, Jungle Jim Lake, and Hangin' Tree, a towering oak used to "execute" countless outlaws.

Driving directions: From Highway 118/Ronald Reagan Freeway in Simi Valley, exit on Kuehner Drive. Drive 1.1 mile south to Smith Road and turn left. Continue 0.4 miles into Corriganville Park and park on the left.

Hiking directions: From the far east end of the parking lot, take the wide trail past the kiosk. The forested trail heads northeast up the draw past coast live oaks and sculpted rock formations on the left. Cross a bridge to a junction. The left fork crosses a wooden bridge, passes a pool, and loops back for a short hike. Stay to the right to the next junction. The right fork is a connector trail to Rocky Peak Park (Hike 25) via a concrete tunnel under the freeway. Curve to the left and cross the stream to another junction. Both trails lead west back to the trailhead. The footpath to the right travels between the sandstone cliffs to a dynamic overlook and a junction. Take the left fork, descending to the old movie sets and the site of Fort Apache. From the sets, cross the bridge back to the parking lot.

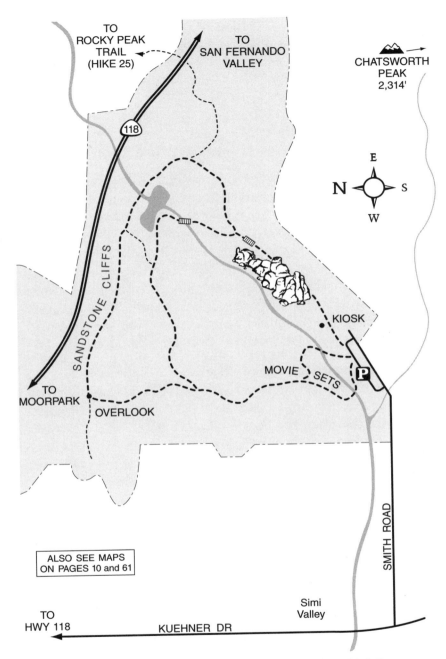

TO
ROCKY PEAK
TRAIL
(HIKE 25)

TO
SAN FERNANDO
VALLEY

CHATSWORTH
PEAK
2,314'

118

E
N — S
W

SANDSTONE CLIFFS

KIOSK

MOVIE SETS

P

TO
MOORPARK

OVERLOOK

ALSO SEE MAPS
ON PAGES 10 and 61

SMITH ROAD

Simi
Valley

TO
HWY 118

KUEHNER DR

CORRIGANVILLE PARK

Hike 27
Sage Ranch Loop Trail

Hiking distance: 2.6 mile loop
Hiking time: 1.3 hours
Elevation gain: 300 feet
Maps: U.S.G.S. Calabasas
       Santa Monica Mountains Conservancy: Sage Ranch Park

Summary of hike: Sage Ranch sits at 2,000 feet and has a garden-of-the-gods appearance. Located in the rocky Simi Hills overlooking the valley, this 635-acre park is rich with world-class sandstone formations. The ranch is an inter-mountain habitat linkage connecting the Simi Hills with the Santa Monica and Santa Susana Mountains. The park boasts an endless display of unique boulders and tilted sandstone outcroppings. Sandstone Ridge, a long, steep, weathered formation with caves and natural sculptures, rises 300 feet from this loop trail. Beautiful carved boulders and eucalyptus trees fill the canyon.

Driving directions: From Highway 118/Ronald Reagan Freeway in the San Fernando Valley, exit on Topanga Canyon Boulevard. Drive south and turn right on Plummer Street. Continue 2.4 miles to Woolsey Canyon Road and turn right. (Along the way, Plummer Street becomes Valley Circle Boulevard and Lake Manor Drive.) Continue on Woolsey Canyon Road 2.4 miles to Black Canyon Road and turn right. The Sage Ranch parking lot is 0.2 miles ahead on the left.

From Ventura Freeway/Highway 101 in the San Fernando Valley, exit on Valley Circle Boulevard. Drive north to Woolsey Canyon Road and turn left.

Hiking directions: From the parking lot, hike west up the park service road. Proceed through the gate, passing orange groves on both sides. At the top of the hill next to the sandstone formations, the trail leaves the paved road and takes the gravel road to the right (north). Continue past a meadow dotted with oak trees and through an enormous garden of sandstone rocks. Watch for a short path on the right to a vista point overlooking Simi Valley. Back on the main trail, the trail parallels Sandstone Ridge before descending into the canyon. Once in the canyon, the trail curves back to the east past another series of large rock formations. Near the east end of the canyon is a trail split. Take the left fork, heading uphill and out of the canyon, back to the parking lot.

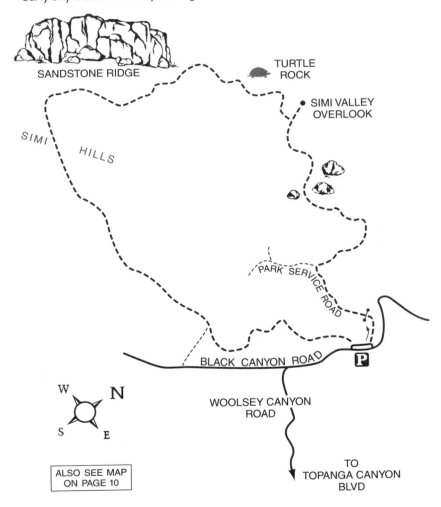

SANDSTONE RIDGE

TURTLE ROCK

SIMI VALLEY OVERLOOK

SIMI HILLS

PARK SERVICE ROAD

BLACK CANYON ROAD

P

WOOLSEY CANYON ROAD

W N S E

ALSO SEE MAP ON PAGE 10

TO TOPANGA CANYON BLVD

SAGE RANCH LOOP TRAIL

Hike 28
Escondido Falls

Hiking distance: 4.2 miles round trip
Hiking time: 2 hours
Elevation gain: 300 feet
Maps: U.S.G.S. Point Dume
     Santa Monica Mountains East Trail Map

Summary of hike: Escondido Falls is a 200-foot multi-tiered cataract deep within the Escondido Canyon Natural Area. The upper cascade can be spotted during the hike, but the trail ends at the base of the lower falls in a box canyon. The falls tumbles 50 feet into a shallow pool, cascading off limestone cliffs into a mossy fern grotto. The hike to the falls begins on a winding, paved residential road due to trail access problems. In less than a mile, a footpath descends into the forested canyon. In the shade of oaks, willows, and sycamores, the canyon trail follows a year-round creek to the waterfall.

Driving directions: From Santa Monica, drive 16.5 miles northbound on the Pacific Coast Highway/Highway 1 to Winding Way and turn right. (Winding Way is 4.5 miles past Malibu Canyon Road.) The signed parking lot is on the left side of Winding Way.

Hiking directions: Hike north up Winding Way past some beautiful homes and ocean vistas on the south-facing slope. At 0.8 miles, leave the road on the well-defined trail, crossing the meadow to the left. Hike downhill into Escondido Canyon and cross the creek. After crossing, take the left fork upstream. (The right fork leads to Latigo Canyon.) Continue up the nearly level canyon trail beside the creek. The forested trail crosses the creek a few more times. After the fifth crossing, Escondido Falls comes into view. The trail ends by a shallow pool surrounded by travertine rock at the base of the waterfall. Return by reversing your route. (The upper falls is on private property and access is not permitted.)

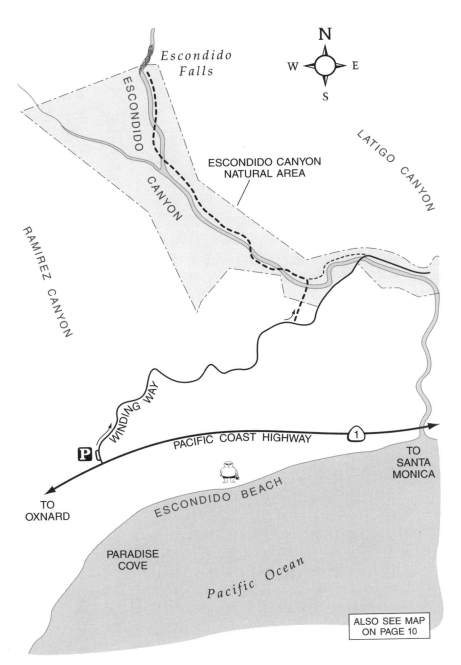

ESCONDIDO CANYON
NATURAL AREA

Escondido
Falls

ESCONDIDO CANYON

LATIGO CANYON

RAMIREZ CANYON

N
W E
S

WINDING WAY

P

PACIFIC COAST HIGHWAY ①

TO
OXNARD

TO
SANTA
MONICA

ESCONDIDO BEACH

PARADISE
COVE

Pacific Ocean

ALSO SEE MAP
ON PAGE 10

ESCONDIDO FALLS

Hike 29
Rising Sun—Solstice Canyon Loop
SOLSTICE CANYON

Hiking distance: 2.8-mile loop
Hiking time: 1.5 hours
Elevation gain: 400 feet
Maps: U.S.G.S. Point Dume and Malibu Beach
N.P.S. Solstice Canyon map
Santa Monica Mountains East Trail Map

Summary of hike: The hike up Solstice Canyon leads to Tropical Terrace, the ruins of a home built in the 1950s and destroyed by fire in 1982. The stone courtyard, garden terraces, stairways, and exotic tropical plants still remain. Near the ruins is Solstice Canyon Falls cascading 30 feet over sandstone rocks. The Rising Sun Trail traverses the east wall of Solstice Canyon. The undulating path overlooks the lush canyon to the Pacific Ocean. The hike returns along the canyon floor parallel to Solstice Creek, passing through oak and walnut groves, grassy meadows, and picnic areas.

Driving directions: From Santa Monica, drive 14.3 miles northbound on the Pacific Coast Highway/Highway 1 to Corral Canyon Road and turn right. (Corral Canyon Road is 2.3 miles past Malibu Canyon Road.) Continue 0.2 miles to the gated entrance on the left. Turn left and drive 0.3 miles to the parking lot at road's end.

Hiking directions: Hike north up the steps past the TRW Trailhead sign. Wind up the hillside to a service road. Take the road uphill to the right to the TRW buildings, now home for the Santa Monica Mountains Conservancy. The Rising Sun Trail begins to the right of the second building. Long, wide switchbacks lead up to the east ridge of Solstice Canyon. Follow the ridge north towards the back of the canyon, and descend through lush vegetation. At the canyon floor, cross the creek to the ruins. Take the path upstream to the waterfalls and pools. After exploring, return on the service road parallel to Solstice Creek. A half mile down canyon is the Keller House, a stone cottage built in 1865. Bear left at a road split, cross a wooden bridge, and return to the trailhead.

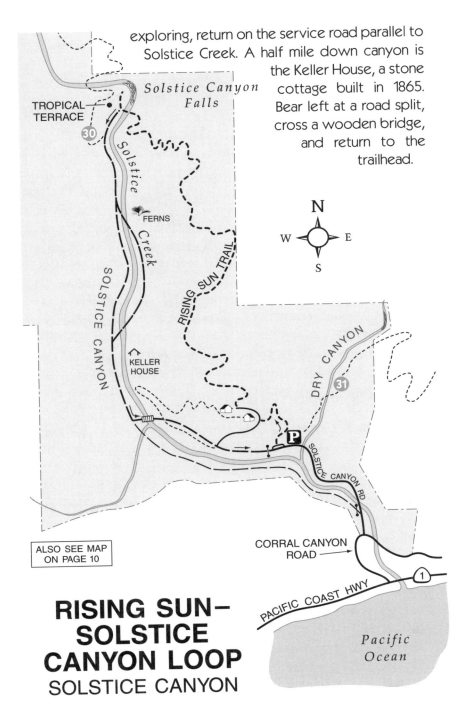

ALSO SEE MAP
ON PAGE 10

RISING SUN–
SOLSTICE
CANYON LOOP
SOLSTICE CANYON

Hike 30
Sostomo—Deer Valley Loop
SOLSTICE CANYON

Hiking distance: 6.2 miles round trip
Hiking time: 3 hours
Elevation gain: 1,100 feet
Maps: U.S.G.S. Point Dume
      N.P.S. Solstice Canyon map
      Santa Monica Mountains East Trail Map

Summary of hike: The Sostomo-Deer Valley Loop ascends the west wall of Solstice Canyon to a 1,200-foot ridge. The trail winds through chaparral and coastal sage with stream crossings, oak woodlands, and grassy meadows. Sweeping vistas above Point Dume extend across Santa Monica Bay. The Sostomo–Deer Valley Loop is accessed by the Solstice Canyon Trail (Hike 29), which follows Solstice Creek along the canyon floor through meadows, picnic areas, oak and walnut groves, and past the historic Keller House, a stone building dating back to 1865.

Driving directions: Same as Hike 29.

Hiking directions: Take the posted Solstice Canyon Trail, and follow the paved road under sycamore trees alongside the creek. Cross a wood bridge to the west side of the creek at 0.2 miles. Continue up canyon past the historic Keller House. Just beyond the house is a trail split. The right fork leaves the main road and meanders through an oak grove, crossing the creek twice before rejoining the road. At 1.2 miles, just shy of the Tropical Terrace, is the posted Sostomo Trail. Bear left on the footpath, and begin ascending the west canyon wall. Climb at a moderate grade to magnificent views of Solstice Canyon. Rock hop over the creek in a narrow gorge. Wind up the canyon wall, passing the remnants of a home and chimney. At the head of the canyon is a towering sedimentary rock monolith. The trail skirts the park boundary and curves left before reaching the spectacular outcropping. Cross the creek again, passing the shell of a sturdy rock house. Climb to a junction with the Deer Valley Loop. Begin the loop to the right, leading to an open, grassy flat where the trail levels off. At an unpaved road, bear left for 50 yards and return to the footpath on the left. The sweeping coastal views extend across Santa Monica Bay, including a bird's-eye view of Point Dume. Switchback sharply left at the trail sign, and return on the lower loop. The Rising Sun Trail (Hike 29) can be seen across the canyon. Complete the loop and return by retracing your steps.

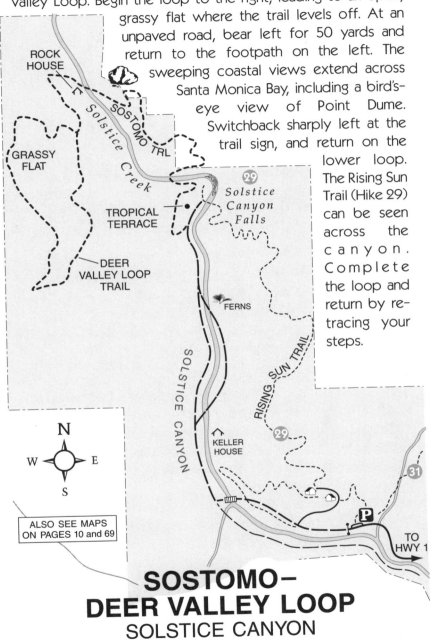

SOSTOMO–
DEER VALLEY LOOP
SOLSTICE CANYON

Hike 31
Dry Canyon Trail to waterfall
SOLSTICE CANYON

Hiking distance: 1.2 miles round trip
Hiking time: 30 minutes
Elevation gain: 200 feet
Maps: U.S.G.S. Malibu Beach
N.P.S. Solstice Canyon map
Santa Monica Mountains East Trail Map

Summary of hike: The Dry Canyon Trail leads up a canyon filled with oaks and sycamore to an overlook of a seasonal, free-falling waterfall. After a rain, when the fall is active, the long, slender waterfall drops 200 feet off the hillside cliff.

Driving directions: From Santa Monica, drive 14.3 miles northbound on the Pacific Coast Highway/Highway 1 to Corral Canyon Road and turn right. (Corral Canyon Road is 2.3 miles past Malibu Canyon Road.) Continue 0.2 miles to the gated entrance on the left. Turn left, entering the park, and drive 0.3 miles to the parking lot at road's end.

Hiking directions: From the parking area, hike 20 yards back down the road to the signed Dry Canyon Trail on the left. Head north up the side canyon into a grassy oak grove. The well-defined trail parallels and crosses the creek. As you near the falls, the trail gains more elevation. The falls is across the narrow canyon on the left. This overlook is our turnaround spot. Return along the same path.

To hike further, the trail continues a short distance to the end of the canyon before switchbacks lead up the canyon wall to Corral Canyon Road. Beyond the waterfall, the trail is not maintained and becomes overgrown with brush.

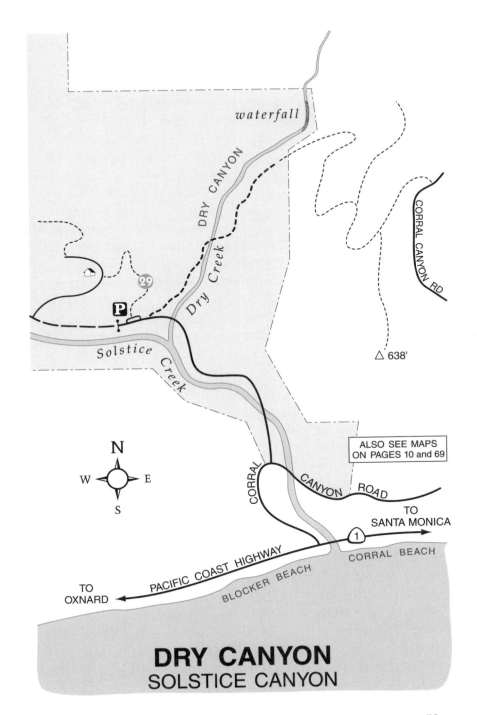

waterfall

DRY CANYON

Dry Creek

CORRAL CANYON RD

29

P

△ 638'

Solstice Creek

ALSO SEE MAPS
ON PAGES 10 and 69

N
W ◇ E
S

CORRAL CANYON ROAD

TO
SANTA MONICA

1

TO
OXNARD

PACIFIC COAST HIGHWAY

BLOCKER BEACH

CORRAL BEACH

DRY CANYON
SOLSTICE CANYON

Hike 32
Peter Strauss Ranch

OPEN DAILY: 8 A.M.—5 P.M.

Hiking distance: 1 mile loop
Hiking time: 30 minutes
Elevation gain: 200 feet
Maps: U.S.G.S. Point Dume
N.P.S. Peter Strauss Ranch Site
Santa Monica Mountains East Trail Map

Summary of hike: Triunfo Creek flows through the 65-acre Peter Strauss Ranch with tree-shaded picnic areas along the wide creekside lawns. This hike parallels the creek through an enchanting refuge. The trail traverses the hillside terraces above the creek through eucalyptus, oak, bay and sycamore groves, and a lush understory of ferns and poison oak. The ranch has a giant outdoor aviary, amphitheater, and a 1926 stone house.

Driving directions: From Santa Monica, drive 12 miles northbound on the Pacific Coast Highway/Highway 1 to Malibu Canyon Road. Turn right and drive 6.5 miles to Mulholland Highway. Turn left and drive 5.1 miles to the park entrance on the left.

From the Ventura Freeway/Highway 101 in Agoura Hills, exit on Kanan Road. Head 3 miles south to Troutdale Drive. Turn left and drive 0.4 miles to Mulholland Highway. Turn left and immediately turn right into the Peter Strauss Park entrance and parking lot.

Hiking directions: Take the footpath towards Mulholland Highway and the entrance arch. Cross the bridge spanning Triunfo Creek, and enter the park on the service road to the left, across from Troutdale Drive. Head south past the amphitheater to the end of the service road by the old Lake Enchanto Dam, built in the 1940s. Stay to the left, parallel to Triunfo Creek. The forested Peter Strauss Trail traverses the hillside above the creek to a junction. Take the right fork up a series of switchbacks. At the top, the trail levels out and heads west. At the west end, switchbacks zigzag down the slope. Pass small meadows and cross a wooden bridge to a junction. The right fork leads to a picnic area. The left fork completes the loop at the amphitheater and aviary.

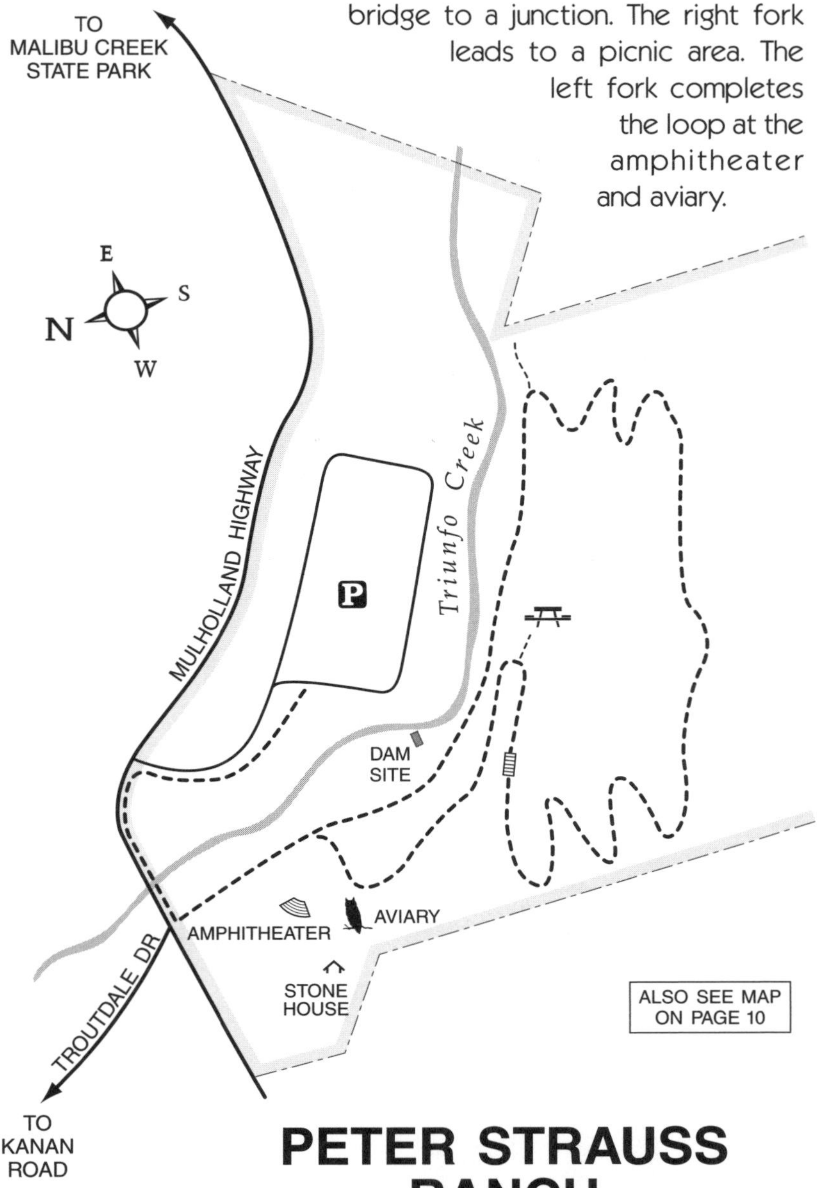

TO
MALIBU CREEK
STATE PARK

E
S
N
W

MULHOLLAND HIGHWAY

Triunfo Creek

P

DAM
SITE

AMPHITHEATER

AVIARY

STONE
HOUSE

TROUTDALE DR

ALSO SEE MAP
ON PAGE 10

TO
KANAN
ROAD

PETER STRAUSS RANCH

Hike 33
Paramount Ranch

Hiking distance: 2.75 miles round trip
Hiking time: 1.5 hours
Elevation gain: 200 feet
Maps: U.S.G.S. Point Dume
N.P.S. Paramount Ranch Site map
Santa Monica Mountains East Trail Map

Summary of hike: Paramount Ranch has a diverse and scenic landscape with oak savannahs, chaparral-covered hillsides, canyons, creekside thickets, rolling grasslands and the prominent Sugarloaf Peak overlooking the parkland. The historic 326-acre ranch has been a motion picture filming site for hundreds of movies and television shows, including *Dr. Quinn, Medicine Woman*; *Have Gun Will Travel*; *The Cisco Kid*; *The Rifleman*; and *Tom Sawyer*. The hike takes in two loop trails within the ranch that represent the diverse terrain. The Medea Creek Trail parallels the year-round creek through a riparian zone and circles an 860-foot hill near Sugarloaf Mountain. The Coyote Canyon Trail climbs the chaparral-covered canyon to a panorama of the ranch and an overlook of the mountains to the west. To reach the trail, wander through the streets of the realistic western town movie set with false store fronts, saloons and hotels.

Driving directions: From Santa Monica, drive 12 miles northbound on the Pacific Coast Highway/Highway 1 to Malibu Canyon Road. Turn right and continue 6.5 miles to Mulholland Highway. Turn left and drive 3.2 miles to Cornell Road. Turn right and drive 0.4 miles to the Paramount Ranch entrance on the left. Turn left and continue 0.2 miles to the parking area.

From the Ventura Freeway/Highway 101 in Agoura Hills, exit on Kanan Road. Head 0.4 miles south to Cornell Road and turn left. Drive 1.8 miles to the ranch entrance on the right.

Hiking directions: COYOTE CANYON TRAIL—1.75 MILE LOOP: Cross the bridge over Medea Creek, and walk through Western

Town to the signed Coyote Canyon Trail. Head west up the small ravine to a junction. The left fork is the half-mile Overlook Trail. The right (northeast) fork follows the ridgeline to another junction—the left fork leads to a picnic area, and the right fork heads down to a paved road. Return through Western Town.

MEDEA CREEK AND RUN TRAIL—1 MILE LOOP: From the parking area, head south on the service road parallel to Medea Creek. Take the signed trail bearing left. Switchbacks lead up to a junction. Continue straight ahead on the Run Trail to a trail split. Bear left towards Sugarloaf Peak. Curve to the right above the meadow at the base of the mountain. Descend into the wooded area parallel to Medea Creek, returning to the trailhead.

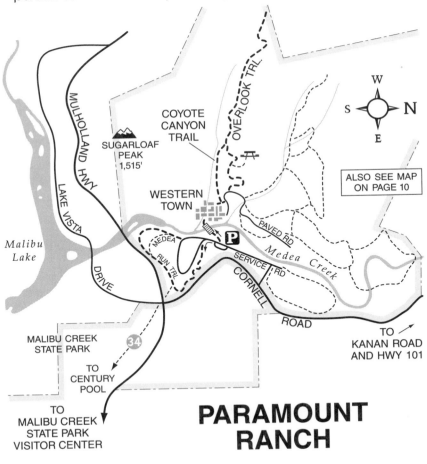

PARAMOUNT RANCH

Hike 34
Reagan Ranch
MALIBU CREEK STATE PARK

Hiking distance: 3 miles round trip
Hiking time: 1.5 hours
Elevation gain: Level
Maps: U.S.G.S. Malibu Beach
      Malibu Creek State Park map
      Santa Monica Mountains East Trail Map

Summary of hike: The Reagan Ranch was President Ronald Reagan's home in the 1950s and 1960s before he was elected governor of California. The 305-acre ranch now occupies the northwest corner of Malibu Creek State Park. A network of trails, once used as horse riding paths for the Reagans, connects the ranch to the heart of the state park. This hike, the Yearling-Deer Leg Loop, includes a duck pond, a large rolling meadow, oak groves, stream crossings, magnificent vistas, and a visit to the Reagan barn.

Driving directions: From Santa Monica, drive 12 miles northbound on the Pacific Coast Highway/Highway 1 to Malibu Canyon Road. Turn right and continue 6.5 miles up this beautiful winding canyon road to Mulholland Highway. Turn left and drive 3.2 miles to Cornell Road. Turn left again and immediately park along the road wherever you find a spot.

From the Ventura Freeway/Highway 101, exit at the Kanan Road off-ramp. Drive south 0.4 miles to Cornell Road. Turn left and continue 2.2 miles to the intersection of Mulholland Highway. Cross and park along the road.

Hiking directions: Enter the ranch at a gateway through the white rail fence on the southeast corner of Mulholland Highway and Cornell Road. Walk a quarter mile on the unpaved Yearling Road, lined with stately eucalyptus trees, to the old Reagan barn. Continue past the barn to a footpath—the Yearling Trail. The duck pond is on the left. Just beyond the pond is the beginning of the loop. Stay to the left on the Yearling Trail, heading towards the meadow. As you hike through the meadow, there are two side trails on the right that intersect with the Yearling Trail. You may bear right on either trail. They connect with the Deer Leg Trail for the return hike. Follow the Deer Leg Trail on the hillside slope as it winds past large oak trees. Cross Udell Creek and return through the meadow, past the pond, and back to the trailhead.

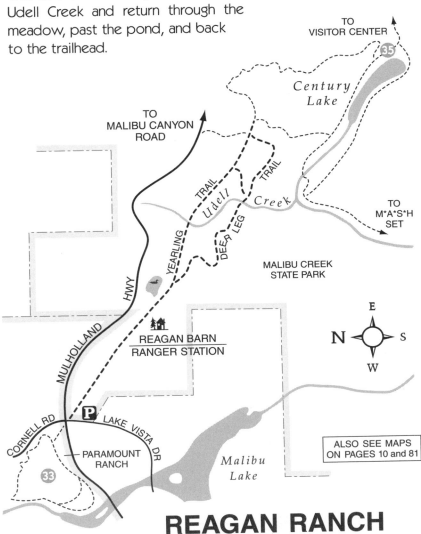

TO
VISITOR CENTER

35

Century Lake

TO
MALIBU CANYON
ROAD

TO
M*A*S*H
SET

TRAIL

Udell *Creek*

TRAIL

YEARLING

DEER LEG

MALIBU CREEK
STATE PARK

HWY

MULHOLLAND

E

N ◆ S

W

REAGAN BARN
RANGER STATION

CORNELL RD

P LAKE VISTA DR

33

PARAMOUNT
RANCH

Malibu Lake

ALSO SEE MAPS
ON PAGES 10 and 81

REAGAN RANCH
MALIBU CREEK STATE PARK

Hike 35
Rock Pool and Century Lake
MALIBU CREEK STATE PARK

Hiking distance: 3 miles round trip
Hiking time: 2 hours
Elevation gain: 300 feet
Maps: U.S.G.S. Malibu Beach
       Malibu Creek State Park Map
       Santa Monica Mountains East Trail Map

Summary of hike: Malibu Creek State Park, purchased by the state from the 20th Century Fox movie studio in 1974, was originally home for thousands of years to the Chumash Indians. The 10,000-acre park contains a visitor center, campground, a manmade 7-acre lake, volcanic rock, sandstone outcroppings, majestic canyons, year-round streams, and over 30 miles of hiking trails that spread over its many acres. This hike follows Malibu Creek to Rock Pool, surrounded by towering volcanic cliffs, and to Century Lake. *Tarzan, Planet of the Apes,* and *South Pacific* have been filmed in the park, to name a few, but it is most recognized for the *M*A*S*H* television series.

Driving directions: From Santa Monica, drive 12 miles northbound on the Pacific Coast Highway/Highway 1 to Malibu Canyon Road. Turn right and continue 6 miles up the winding canyon road. The Malibu Creek State Park entrance is located on the left, shortly before reaching Mulholland Highway. Turn left and park in the second parking lot on the left.
    From the Ventura Freeway/Highway 101, exit at Las Virgenes Road. Head south towards the mountains for 3.5 miles. The Malibu Creek State Park entrance is located on the right, just past Mulholland Highway. Turn right into the park.

Hiking directions: Cross the main road to the trailhead. Follow Crags Road as it slowly curves alongside Malibu Creek to a bridge. Crossing the bridge leads to the visitor center on Crags Road. The High Road stays on the north side of the creek.

Both routes meet at Malibu Creek Bridge. At the bridge, take the posted Gorge Trail south. Bear left along the stream through a lava rock field to Rock Pool at the mouth of the gorge, 0.9 miles from the trailhead.

Return to the main trail back at the bridge. Take Crags Road (the main road) to the northwest. Continue uphill to a trail junction at the crest of the hill. From here you will overlook Century Lake with a great view of Goat Buttes. The trail to the left leads down to the lake. Continuing right on Crags Road leads to the M*A*S*H set one mile ahead. To return, retrace your steps.

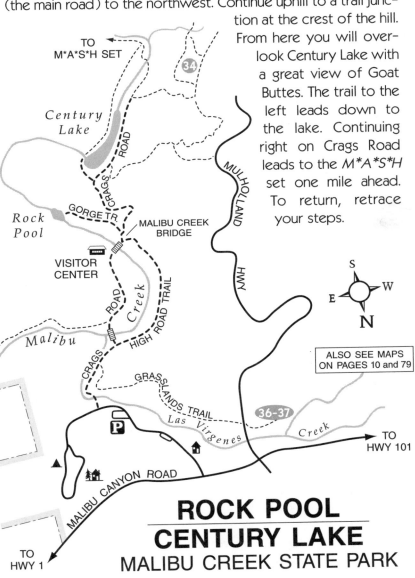

ROCK POOL
CENTURY LAKE
MALIBU CREEK STATE PARK

Hike 36
Liberty Canyon Natural Preserve
MALIBU CREEK STATE PARK

Hiking distance: 3.8 miles round trip
Hiking time: 2 hours
Elevation gain: 100 feet
Maps: U.S.G.S. Malibu Beach and Calabasas
Malibu Creek State Park map
Santa Monica Mountains East Trail Map

Summary of hike: Liberty Canyon is one of three natural preserves in Malibu Creek State Park and is home to a rare stand of California valley oaks. The Grasslands Trail crosses rolling grasslands and merges with the Liberty Canyon Trail at a bridge spanning Liberty Creek. The Liberty Canyon Trail parallels the creek, gently climbing through oak woodlands to the head of the canyon.

Driving directions: From Santa Monica, drive 12 miles northbound on the Pacific Coast Highway/Highway 1 to Malibu Canyon Road. Turn right and continue 6.5 miles up this beautiful, winding canyon road to Mulholland Highway. Turn left and park 0.1 mile ahead in the parking pullouts on either side of the road.
From the Ventura Freeway/Highway 101, take the Las Virgenes Road exit. Drive 3.1 miles south to Mulholland Highway. Turn right and park 0.1 mile ahead in the parking pullouts.

Hiking directions: Begin on the signed Grasslands Trail, heading north past a white adobe house on the left. Cross the rolling grasslands, looping around the west side of an Edison substation. Continue north past oak trees, bearing right at a trail split. Cross a footbridge over Liberty Creek by a small waterfall and pools to a signed junction. Head left on the Liberty Canyon Trail past a junction at one mile with the Talepop Trail (Hike 37). Continue straight ahead, climbing the hillside through an oak grove overlooking the canyon, then return to the canyon bottom. The trail ends at the head of the canyon by Park Vista

Road and Liberty Canyon Road. The Phantom Trail heads southwest to the left. Return along the same trail.

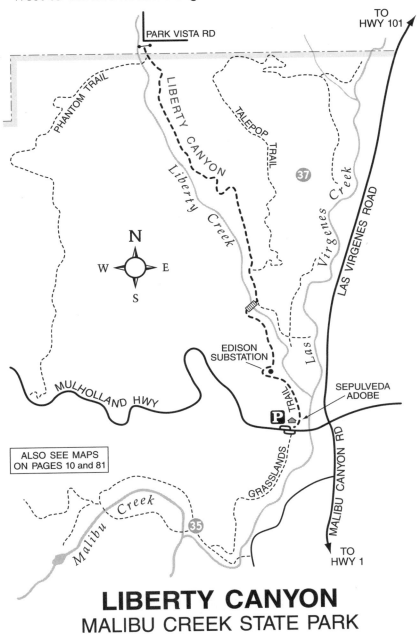

PARK VISTA RD

TO
HWY 101

PHANTOM TRAIL

LIBERTY CANYON

Liberty Creek

TALEPOP TRAIL

37

Las Virgenes Creek

LAS VIRGENES ROAD

N
W E
S

EDISON
SUBSTATION

SEPULVEDA
ADOBE

MULHOLLAND HWY

Las

P

TRAIL

MALIBU CANYON RD

ALSO SEE MAPS
ON PAGES 10 and 81

GRASSLANDS

Creek

35

Malibu Creek

TO
HWY 1

LIBERTY CANYON
MALIBU CREEK STATE PARK

Hike 37
Talepop Trail—Las Virgenes Loop
MALIBU CREEK STATE PARK

Hiking distance: 4.6 miles round trip
Hiking time: 2.5 hours
Elevation gain: 450 feet
Maps: U.S.G.S. Malibu Beach and Calabasas
      Malibu Creek State Park map
      Santa Monica Mountains East Trail Map

Summary of hike: This loop hike begins in Liberty Canyon, a natural preserve in Malibu Creek State Park. The Talepop Trail climbs to a grassy ridge overlooking two canyons, traverses the ridge, and returns in Las Virgenes Canyon parallel to the creek. Talepop Trail is named for a small Chumash Indian village.

Driving directions: Same as Hike 36.

Hiking directions: Take the signed Grasslands Trail, and head north across the rolling meadow. Loop around an Edison substation. Continue north, bearing right at a trail split, to a footbridge over Liberty Creek by rock formations and pools. Cross the bridge to a signed junction. Take the left fork on the Liberty Canyon Trail, beginning the loop. At one mile is a signed junction with the Talepop Trail on the right. Head west on the Talepop Trail, winding up the west canyon wall a half mile to the ridge. Follow the ridge north to the summit, overlooking Liberty Canyon on the west and Las Virgenes Canyon on the east. At the northern park boundary, bear right, down the hillside. Switchbacks lead to the Las Virgenes Canyon floor by Las Virgenes Creek and a junction. The left fork crosses the creek and leads 0.3 miles to De Anza Park. Take the right fork—the Las Virgenes Trail—along the west side of the creek. As you approach White Oak Farm (a private residence), take the signed Liberty Canyon Trail to the right. A short distance ahead is a junction, completing the loop. Bear left on the Grasslands Trail, cross the bridge, and retrace your steps.

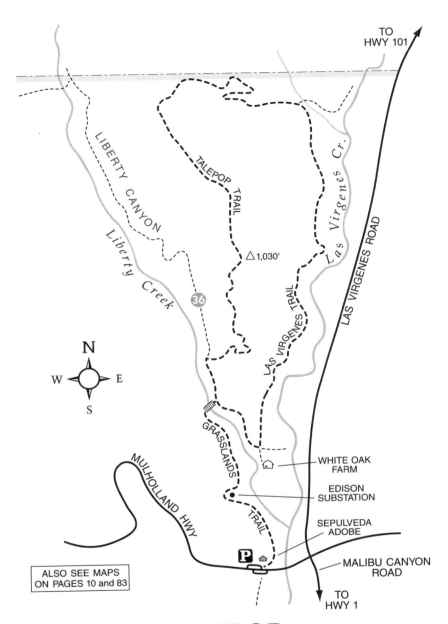

TO
HWY 101

LIBERTY CANYON

Liberty Creek

TALEPOP TRAIL

△1,030'

36

Las Virgenes Cr.

LAS VIRGENES ROAD

LAS VIRGENES TRAIL

N
W   E
S

GRASSLANDS   TRAIL

MULHOLLAND HWY

WHITE OAK
FARM

EDISON
SUBSTATION

SEPULVEDA
ADOBE

P

MALIBU CANYON
ROAD

TO
HWY 1

ALSO SEE MAPS
ON PAGES 10 and 83

TALEPOP–
LAS VIRGENES LOOP
MALIBU CREEK STATE PARK

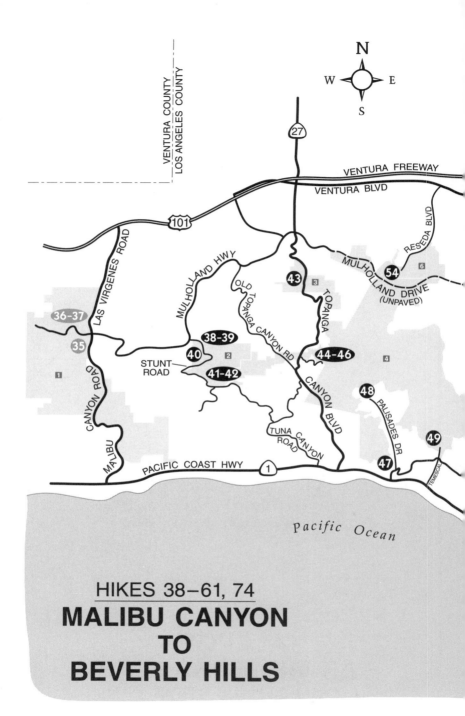

N
W ← ○ → E
S

VENTURA COUNTY
LOS ANGELES COUNTY

27

VENTURA FREEWAY
VENTURA BLVD

101

RESEDA BLVD

MULHOLLAND HWY

OLD TOPANGA CANYON RD

MULHOLLAND DRIVE
(UNPAVED)

54

6

43

3

TOPANGA

LAS VIRGENES ROAD

36-37

35

38-39

40

2

STUNT
ROAD

41-42

44-46

4

CANYON BLVD

48

PALISADES DR

1

MALIBU CANYON ROAD

TUNA CANYON
ROAD

47

49

TEMESCAL

PACIFIC COAST HWY

1

Pacific Ocean

HIKES 38–61, 74

MALIBU CANYON
TO
BEVERLY HILLS

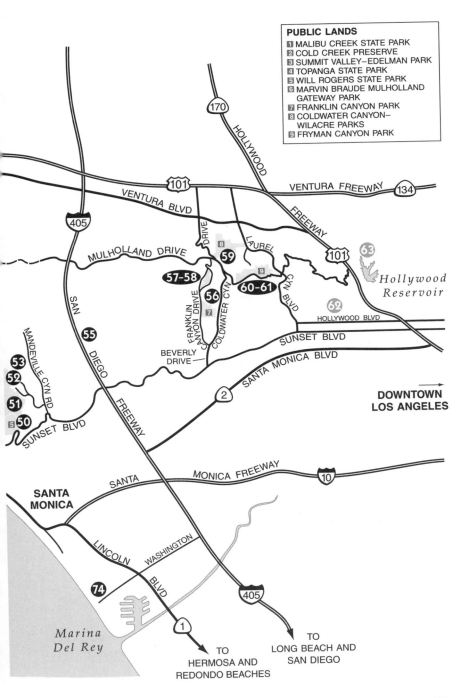

PUBLIC LANDS
1 MALIBU CREEK STATE PARK
2 COLD CREEK PRESERVE
3 SUMMIT VALLEY–EDELMAN PARK
4 TOPANGA STATE PARK
5 WILL ROGERS STATE PARK
6 MARVIN BRAUDE MULHOLLAND GATEWAY PARK
7 FRANKLIN CANYON PARK
8 COLDWATER CANYON–WILACRE PARKS
9 FRYMAN CANYON PARK

Hollywood Reservoir

DOWNTOWN LOS ANGELES

SANTA MONICA

Marina Del Rey

TO HERMOSA AND REDONDO BEACHES

TO LONG BEACH AND SAN DIEGO

Hike 38
Calabasas Peak

Hiking distance: 4 miles round trip
Hiking time: 2 hours
Elevation gain: 900 feet
Maps: U.S.G.S. Malibu Beach
            Santa Monica Mountains East Trail Map

Summary of hike: Calabasas Peak towers over Red Rock Canyon, Old Topanga Canyon and bowl-shaped Cold Creek Canyon. The route to the 2,163-foot peak follows the Calabasas Motorway, a graded fire road. The vehicle-restricted road crosses the head of Red Rock Canyon past magnificent geological formations, including large, weathered sandstone outcroppings and tilted sandstone slabs with long ribs. Along the trail are spectacular 360-degree vistas into the surrounding canyons and the San Fernando Valley.

Driving directions: From Santa Monica, drive 12 miles northbound on the Pacific Coast Highway/Highway 1 to Malibu Canyon Road. Turn right and drive 6.5 miles to Mulholland Highway. Turn right and continue 4 miles to Stunt Road. Turn right again and drive one mile to the pullout on the right.
    From the Ventura Freeway/Highway 101 in Calabasas, exit on Las Virgenes Road. Head 3 miles south to Mulholland Highway. Turn left and go 4 miles to Stunt Road. Turn right and drive one mile to the pullout on the right.

Hiking directions: Cross Stunt Road and walk 20 yards downhill to the trailhead. Walk up the unpaved fire road past the gate. The trail zigzags up the mountain to a junction at 0.7 miles on a saddle at the head of Red Rock Canyon. The right fork heads into Red Rock Canyon (Hike 39). Continue straight ahead to the north along the cliff's edge, passing large eroded sandstone slabs while overlooking Red Rock Canyon. As Calabasas Peak comes into view, the trail curves sharply to the right, circling the peak along an eastern ridge. From the ridge are views into Old Topanga Canyon to the northeast. The trail heads gently downhill before a steep descent. Just before the steep descent, watch for a narrow path on the left. Take this side path west up to the chaparral-covered summit. After lingering at the peak, retrace your steps.

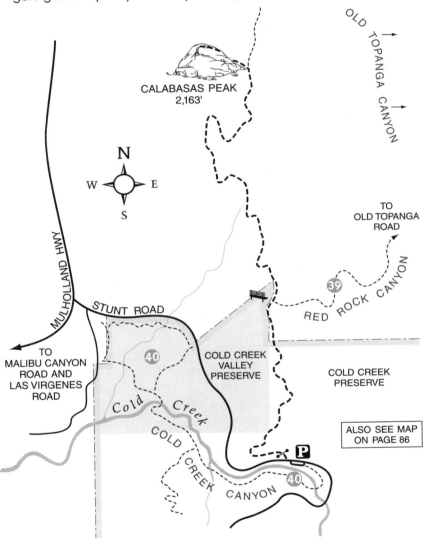

CALABASAS PEAK

Hike 39
Red Rock Canyon

Hiking distance: 4 miles round trip
Hiking time: 2 hours
Elevation gain: 700 feet
Maps: U.S.G.S. Malibu Beach
Santa Monica Mountains East Trail Map

Summary of hike: Red Rock Canyon is a beautiful multi-colored canyon similar to the canyons in the southwest. Huge weather-sculpted red sandstone formations and conglomerate rocks dominate the landscape dotted with oaks and sycamores. Shell fossils can be spotted in the eroded rocks, shallow caves, overhangs, and arches. The riparian canyon is a wildlife corridor connecting Topanga State Park and Malibu Creek State Park. The trail follows the first portion of the Calabasas Motorway, a graded fire road, to the head of Red Rock Canyon.

Driving directions: Same as Hike 38.

Hiking directions: Cross Stunt Road and walk 20 yards west downhill to the trailhead. Take the unpaved road past the gate and wind up the mountain. At 0.7 miles is a junction on a saddle at the head of Red Rock Canyon. The trail straight ahead to the north leads to Calabasas Peak (Hike 38). Take the right fork east into Red Rock Canyon. Continue downhill deeper into the canyon. Pass numerous red sandstone formations to the signed Red Rock Canyon Trail on the left at 1.4 miles. Bear left on the footpath, and walk up wooden steps to the base of some formations. The trail curves up the draw, crosses a seasonal stream, and passes additional sandstone formations along the north wall of the canyon. Continue uphill to the trail's end at an overlook. Return along the same path back to the canyon floor.

Before returning, take a short detour 200 yards to the left on the main trail to an awesome red rock formation with shallow caves and arches. The trail continues a half mile to the Red

Rock Canyon picnic area by Red Rock Road. Return by retracing your steps.

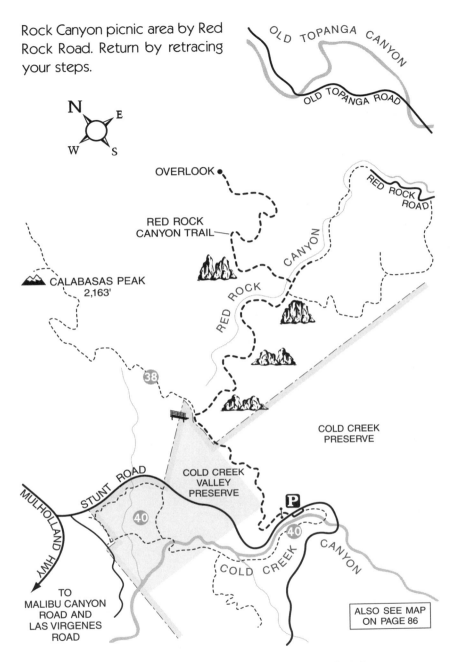

RED ROCK CANYON

Hike 40
Cold Creek Trail
COLD CREEK PRESERVE

Hiking distance: 3 miles round trip
Hiking time: 1.5 hours
Elevation gain: 300 feet
Maps: U.S.G.S. Malibu Beach
 Santa Monica Mountains East Trail Map

Summary of hike: The Cold Creek Valley Preserve sits in a flat bowl set among craggy sandstone peaks. It is home to a wide assortment of plant communities and flowers. Cold Creek flows through the valley preserve and Cold Creek Canyon. The Cold Creek Trail leads to the 57-acre preserve parallel to the creek. The trail meanders through riparian woodlands and a gently rolling grass meadow. En route, the trail crosses the creek three times and traverses the hillside underneath the shade of oaks and sycamores.

Driving directions: Same as Hike 38.

Hiking directions: Take the trail southeast for a short distance, parallel to the road. Curve right and cross Cold Creek. Follow the creek downstream on the Lower Stunt High/Cold Creek Trail, and head into the forested canyon. Cross a tributary stream to a junction at a half mile. The left fork leaves the riparian canopy and heads up the hillside on the Lower Stunt High Trail to Stunt Road. Go to the right on the Cold Creek Trail, staying close to Cold Creek. Continue northwest as the path rises above and returns to the creek. Cross Cold Creek to a junction in the preserve at one mile. This is the beginning of the Deer Grass-Yucca Trail loop within the preserve, which may be hiked in either direction. The loop is one mile, connecting to McKain Street and Stunt Road. After hiking the loop, return on the same path.

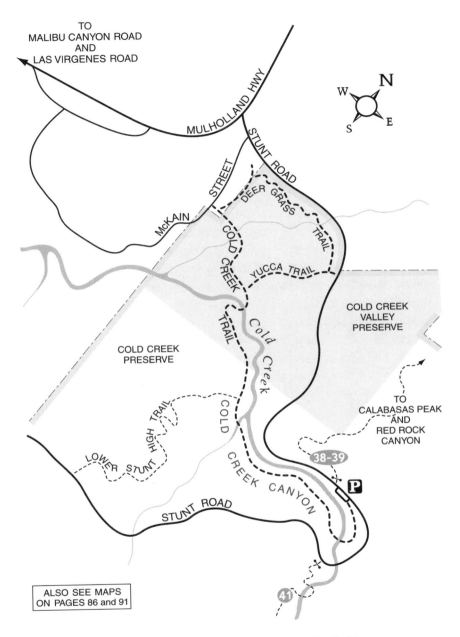

TO
MALIBU CANYON ROAD
AND
LAS VIRGENES ROAD

MULHOLLAND HWY

STUNT ROAD

McKAIN STREET

DEER GRASS TRAIL

COLD CREEK

YUCCA TRAIL

Cold Creek

TRAIL

COLD CREEK
PRESERVE

COLD CREEK
VALLEY
PRESERVE

TO
CALABASAS PEAK
AND
RED ROCK
CANYON

LOWER STUNT HIGH TRAIL

COLD CREEK CANYON

38-39

P

STUNT ROAD

41

N
W   E
S

ALSO SEE MAPS
ON PAGES 86 and 91

COLD CREEK TRAIL
COLD CREEK PRESERVE

Hike 41
Cold Creek Canyon Preserve
A free access permit is required
Contact The Mountains Restoration Trust: (818) 346-9675

Hiking distance: 3.3 miles round trip
Hiking time: 1.5 hours
Elevation gain: 800 feet
Maps: U.S.G.S. Malibu Beach
Santa Monica Mountains East Trail Map

Summary of hike: Cold Creek Canyon is a pristine, bowl-shaped canyon with a year-round creek and a diverse eco-system. The 1,100-acre nature preserve is owned by the Mountains Restoration Trust, a non-profit land trust created to protect and enhance the natural resources of the Santa Monica Mountains. To protect the fragile resources of the preserve, a free access permit is requested. Cold Creek Canyon has high ridges, a steep slope, and magnificent sandstone rock formations. The headwaters of Cold Creek originate within the preserve, rising from springs and cascading down canyon. This hike winds down the north-facing watershed through lush streamside vegetation and jungle-like ferns, passing cascades and small waterfalls. The trail weaves through the natural basin in an idyllic setting under oak, maple, sycamore, and bay woodlands. Watch for the remains of a turn-of-the-century homesteader house, hand-carved into the giant split sandstone boulders.

Driving directions: From Santa Monica, drive 12 northbound on the Pacific Coast Highway/Highway 1 to Malibu Canyon Road and turn right. Drive 6.5 miles to Mulholland Highway. Turn right and continue 4 miles to Stunt Road. Turn right and drive 3.3 miles to the Cold Creek parking pullout on the left, by a chain-link fence. Park off road on the shoulder.

From the Ventura Freeway/Highway 101 in Calabasas, exit on Las Virgenes Road. Head 3 miles south to Mulholland Highway. Turn left and continue 4 miles to Stunt Road. Turn right and drive 3.3 miles to the Cold Creek parking pullout on the left.

Hiking directions: Walk through the gate in the chain-link fence, and head east through the tall chaparral. The trail leads gradually downhill along the contours of the hillside and across a wooden bridge over Cold Creek at 0.6 miles. Pass moss covered rocks and a rusty classic Dodge truck as you make your way into the lush vegetation and open oak woodland to the canyon floor. Cross Cold Creek again and continue past large sandstone boulders to the remains of Herman Hethke's stone house. Several switchbacks lead downhill across side streams and past small waterfalls. At 1.6 miles, the path reaches the locked lower gate at Stunt Road. Return by retracing your steps up canyon.

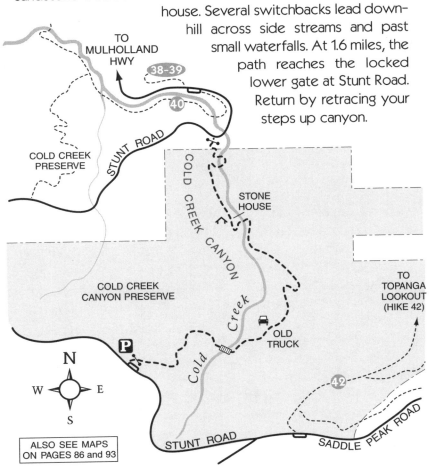

COLD CREEK
CANYON PRESERVE

Hike 42
Topanga Fire Lookout
COLD CREEK CANYON PRESERVE

Hiking distance: 2 miles round trip
Hiking time: 1 hour
Elevation gain: 200 feet
Maps: U.S.G.S. Malibu Beach
　　　　Santa Monica Mountains East Trail Map

Summary of hike: The Topanga Fire Lookout, destroyed in a 1970 fire, was, ironically, used by the fire department to spot fires. All that remains is a large multi-level concrete foundation perched at the edge of the 2,469-foot mountain. The hike to the lookout follows the Topanga Ridge Trail, a fire road along the east ridge of the Cold Creek Canyon Preserve. From the lookout are spectacular views into Old Topanga Canyon, Cold Creek Canyon Preserve, Red Rock Canyon, the expansive San Fernando Valley to Los Angeles, and Santa Monica Bay.

Driving directions: From Santa Monica, drive 12 miles northbound on the Pacific Coast Highway/Highway 1 to Malibu Canyon Road. Turn right and drive 6.5 miles to Mulholland Highway. Turn right and continue 4 miles to Stunt Road. Turn right and drive 5 miles up the winding road to the end of Stunt Road. Turn left on Saddle Peak Road, and park in the pullout on the right.

From the Ventura Freeway/Highway 101 in Calabasas, exit on Las Virgenes Road. Head 3 miles south to Mulholland Highway. Turn left and go 4 miles to Stunt Road. Turn right and drive 4 miles up the road to the end of Stunt Road. Turn left on Saddle Peak Road, and park in the pullout on the right.

Hiking directions: From the parking pullout, cross Saddle Peak Road to the gated service road. Head northeast on the paved road along the ridge, high above Cold Creek Canyon. Calabasas Peak (Hike 38) can be seen to the north. At a quarter mile is a road split. The paved right fork leads to a radar tower.

Bear left on the wide, unpaved path and continue gradually uphill. At one mile is the concrete foundation at the mountain's edge, overlooking Hondo Canyon, Old Topanga Canyon, the Cold Creek drainage, the San Fernando Valley, and sections of Los Angeles. Return by retracing your steps.

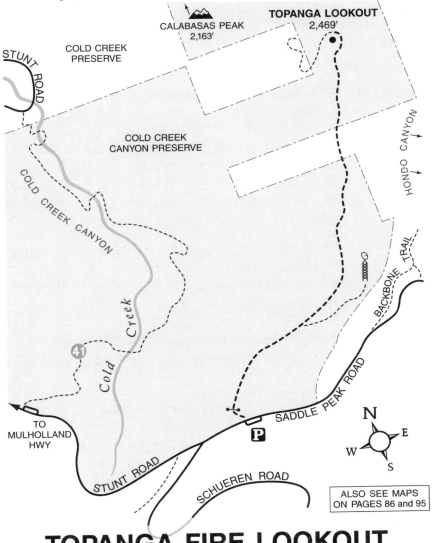

TOPANGA FIRE LOOKOUT
COLD CREEK CANYON PRESERVE

Hike 43
Summit Valley Trail
EDMUND D. EDELMAN PARK

Hiking distance: 2 miles round trip
Hiking time: 1 hour
Elevation gain: 300 feet
Maps: U.S.G.S. Canoga Park
       Santa Monica Mountains East Trail Map

Summary of hike: Edmund D. Edelman Park is located in bowl-shaped Summit Valley at the head of Topanga Canyon. The 1,500-foot ridge at the north end of this 662-acre park separates rural Topanga Canyon from the urban San Fernando Valley. The park's wildlife corridor includes oak woodlands, mixed chaparral communities, native grasslands, and the head-waters of Topanga Creek. This hike loops through two valleys, crosses the gently rolling hills, and parallels Topanga Creek.

Driving directions: From Santa Monica, drive 4 miles north-bound on the Pacific Coast Highway/Highway 1 to Topanga Canyon Boulevard and turn right. Continue 8.2 miles to the signed "Summit Valley/Edmund D. Edelman Park" parking area on the left.

From the Ventura Freeway/Highway 101 in Woodland Hills, exit on Topanga Canyon Boulevard, and drive 4 miles south to the parking area on the right.

Hiking directions: Head west past the trailhead gate, and descend into the forested stream-fed draw, crossing the head-waters of Topanga Creek. At 0.2 miles is a five-way junction. Take the far right trail—the Summit Valley Canyon Trail—to begin the loop. Head north along the canyon floor parallel to the seasonal Topanga Creek on the right. At one mile, just before descending into a eucalyptus grove, the unsigned Summit Valley Loop Trail bears left. Take this trail as it zigzags up the hillside. Heading south, traverse the edge of the hill to a ridge and a junction. (For a shorter hike, the left fork returns to

the five-way junction along the ridge.)
Take the middle fork straight ahead, and
descend into the next drainage. The trail
curves south, returning down the draw
to the five-way junction.

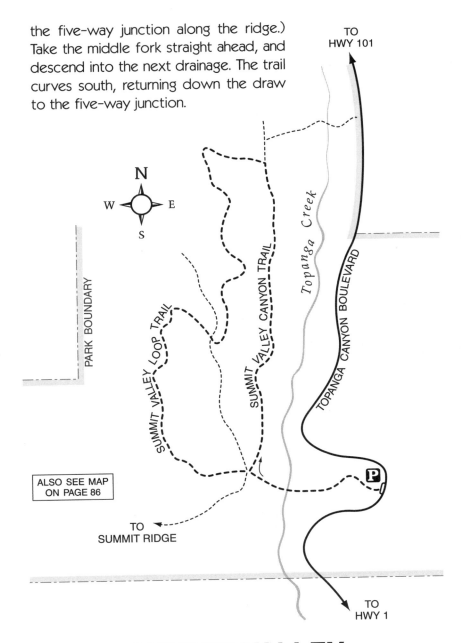

SUMMIT VALLEY
EDMUND D. EDELMAN PARK

Hike 44
Dead Horse Trail
TOPANGA STATE PARK

Hiking distance: 2.5 miles round trip
Hiking time: 1.5 hours
Elevation gain: 400 feet
Maps: U.S.G.S. Topanga
  Santa Monica Mountains East Trail Map

Summary of hike: The Dead Horse Trail in Topanga State Park begins at Trippet Ranch, the park headquarters. The trail crosses rolling grasslands, enters a riparian forest, and descends into a streamside oak woodland. The path crosses a rustic wooden bridge over Trippet Creek in a rocky grotto.

Driving directions: From Santa Monica, drive 4 miles northbound on the Pacific Coast Highway/Highway 1 to Topanga Canyon Boulevard and turn right. Continue 4.6 miles to Entrada Road on the right and turn right again. Drive 0.7 miles and turn left, following the posted state park signs. Turn left again in 0.3 miles into the Topanga State Park parking lot.

From the Ventura Freeway/Highway 101 in Woodland Hills, exit on Topanga Canyon Boulevard, and drive 7.6 miles south to Entrada Drive. Turn left and follow the posted state park signs to the parking lot.

Hiking directions: Take the signed Musch Trail for 50 yards, heading north to a pond on the right. The Dead Horse Trail heads left (west) across from the pond. The footpath parallels a wood rail fence, rolling grasslands, and an oak woodland. At 0.5 miles is a trail split. Take the right fork along the contours of the ridge. The trail descends into a shady riparian forest of bay and sycamore trees. A wooden bridge crosses the rocky streambed of Trippet Creek in a narrow draw. After crossing, steps lead up to a junction. Take the middle fork downhill to a trail split. Bear right and loop around to the lower parking lot near Topanga Canyon Boulevard. Return by retracing your steps.

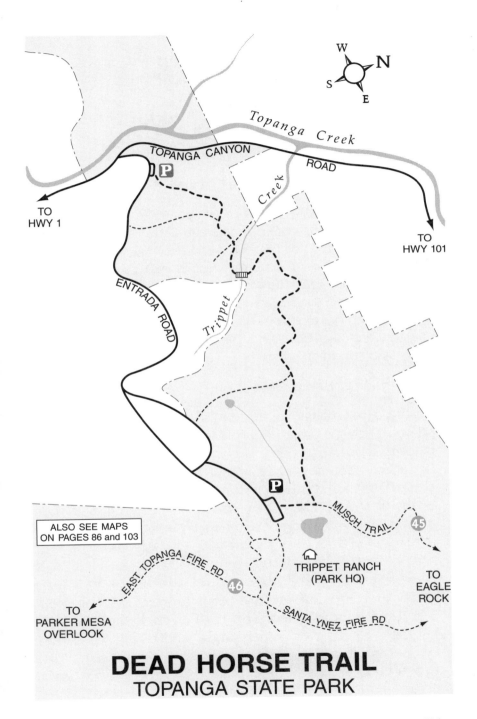

TO
HWY 1

TO
HWY 101

Topanga Creek

TOPANGA CANYON ROAD

P

Creek

ENTRADA ROAD

Trippet

Creek

P

MUSCH TRAIL

45

ALSO SEE MAPS
ON PAGES 86 and 103

EAST TOPANGA FIRE RD.

46

TRIPPET RANCH
(PARK HQ)

SANTA YNEZ FIRE RD.

TO
EAGLE
ROCK

TO
PARKER MESA
OVERLOOK

DEAD HORSE TRAIL
TOPANGA STATE PARK

Hike 45
Eagle Rock Loop
TOPANGA STATE PARK

Hiking distance: 4 miles round trip
Hiking time: 2.5 hours
Elevation gain: 800 feet
Maps: U.S.G.S. Topanga
    Santa Monica Mountains East Trail Map

Summary of hike: This hike begins at a beautiful picnic area with a pond and a one-mile nature trail at Trippet Ranch in Topanga State Park. The hike follows a fire road through grass-lands and oak groves up to Eagle Rock, an impressive sandstone rock pitted with crevices and caves. The views of the mountains, valleys, and the Santa Ynez Canyon are superb. The return on the Musch Trail descends past oak, sycamore, and bay trees. The footpath includes lush vegetation, ferns, moss-covered rocks, and stream crossings.

Driving directions: Same as Hike 44.

Hiking directions: The trailhead is located at the end of the parking lot by the picnic area. Follow the trail uphill a short distance to a posted junction. Take the left trail—the Santa Ynez Fire Road (also known as Eagle Springs Fire Road). Continue along this gradual uphill trail, passing the Santa Ynez Canyon Trail on the right at 0.5 miles. One mile further is the Musch Trail on the left. Follow the ridge a short distance to a trail fork. Bear left to Eagle Rock ,which is close and visually prominent at the head of Santa Ynez Canyon.

After exploring the caves and hollows of the rock and enjoying the 360-degree views, return to the Musch Trail junction. Take the footpath to the right as it winds down to the valley. Cross a couple of ravines through lush foliage and dense oak, sycamore, and laurel woodlands. One mile down this trail is a junction at Musch Camp. Follow the trail sign and walk across the meadow. Turn left a short distance ahead at an unmarked junction and left again at a second unmarked junction. The trail winds back down to the Topanga parking lot, passing a pond along the way.

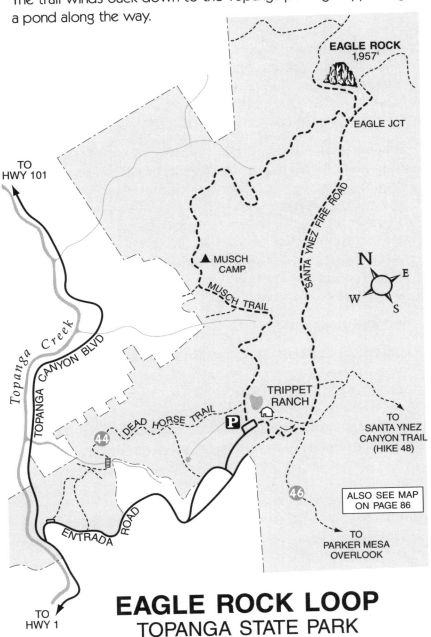

EAGLE ROCK
1,957'

EAGLE JCT

TO
HWY 101

SANTA YNEZ FIRE ROAD

MUSCH CAMP

MUSCH TRAIL

N
E
W
S

Topanga Creek

TOPANGA CANYON BLVD

DEAD HORSE TRAIL

P

44

TRIPPET RANCH

TO
SANTA YNEZ
CANYON TRAIL
(HIKE 48)

46

ALSO SEE MAP
ON PAGE 86

ENTRADA ROAD

TO
PARKER MESA
OVERLOOK

TO
HWY 1

EAGLE ROCK LOOP
TOPANGA STATE PARK

Hike 46
Parker Mesa Overlook
from TOPANGA STATE PARK

Hiking distance: 6 miles round trip
Hiking time: 3 hours
Elevation gain: 800 feet
Maps: U.S.G.S. Topanga
           Santa Monica Mountains East Trail Map

Summary of hike: This hike follows the East Topanga Fire Road along the ridge dividing Topanga Canyon and Santa Ynez Canyon. There are spectacular views into both canyons, including numerous ravines and enormous slabs of sandstone. This hike begins in Topanga State Park at Trippet Ranch (the park headquarters) and heads south. The trail leads to Parker Mesa Overlook, a barren knoll overlooking Topanga Beach, Santa Monica Bay, Pacific Palisades, and Santa Monica. The overlook can also be accessed from the south (Hike 47).

Driving directions: Same as Hike 44.

Hiking directions: Head southeast on the signed trail towards Eagle Rock to a fire road. Bear left up the road to a junction at 0.2 miles. The left fork leads to Eagle Rock (Hike 45). Take the right fork on the East Topanga Fire Road past a grove of coastal oaks. Continue uphill to a ridge and a bench with panoramic views from Topanga Canyon to the Pacific Ocean. A short distance ahead, the trail crosses a narrow ridge overlooking Santa Ynez Canyon and its tilted sandstone slabs. Follow the ridge south, with alternating views of both canyons. At 2.5 miles is a junction with a trail on the right. The main trail (left) leads to Paseo Miramar (Hike 47). Leave the fire road, and take the right trail a half mile to Parker Mesa Overlook at the trail's end. After enjoying the views, return to Trippet Ranch along the same route.

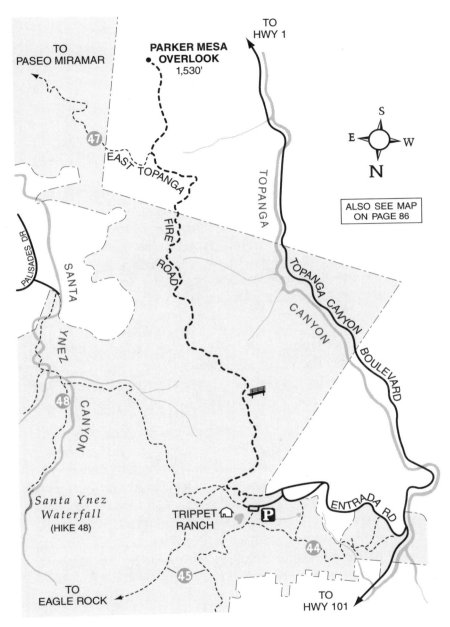

TO
PASEO MIRAMAR

TO
HWY 1

**PARKER MESA
OVERLOOK**
1,530'

47

EAST TOPANGA

FIRE ROAD

TOPANGA

TOPANGA CANYON BOULEVARD

CANYON

PALISADES DR

SANTA

YNEZ

CANYON

48

ALSO SEE MAP
ON PAGE 86

S
E ⊕ W
N

*Santa Ynez
Waterfall*
(HIKE 48)

TRIPPET
RANCH

P

ENTRADA RD

44

45

TO
EAGLE ROCK

TO
HWY 101

PARKER MESA OVERLOOK
from TOPANGA STATE PARK

Hike 47
Parker Mesa Overlook
from PASEO MIRAMAR

Hiking distance: 5 miles round trip
Hiking time: 2.5 hours
Elevation gain: 1,200 feet
Maps: U.S.G.S. Topanga
       Santa Monica Mountains East Trail Map

Summary of hike: The hike to Parker Mesa Overlook from Paseo Miramar has spectacular vistas along the trail. The trail follows a ridge separating Santa Ynez Canyon and Los Liones Canyon. There are views from Venice to Malibu and from West Los Angeles to Topanga. The Parker Mesa Overlook (also known as the Topanga Overlook) is a barren knoll overlooking Santa Monica Bay to Palos Verdes and, on clear days, Catalina Island.

Driving directions: From Santa Monica, drive 3 miles northbound on the Pacific Coast Highway/Highway 1 to Sunset Boulevard. Turn right and drive 0.3 miles to Paseo Miramar. Turn left and drive about one mile to the end of the road and park.

Hiking directions: Hike north past the fire road gate as the road climbs along the ridge. Pass the Los Liones Trail on the left. Continue along the hillside overlooking Santa Ynez Canyon to a junction at two miles. Leave the fire road and take the trail to the left, heading south. The trail ends a half mile ahead at the Parker Mesa Overlook, a bald knoll overlooking the Pacific Ocean. (The main fire road leads 2.5 miles further to Trippet Ranch—Hike 46.) After enjoying the views at the overlook, return along the same trail.

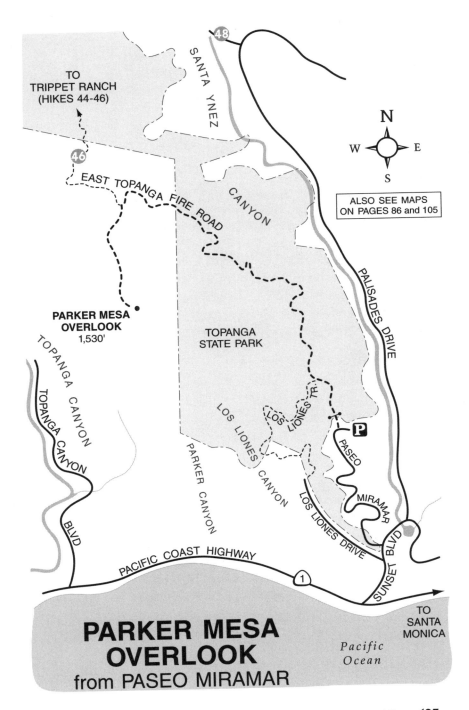

48

TO
TRIPPET RANCH
(HIKES 44-46)

SANTA YNEZ

46

EAST TOPANGA FIRE ROAD

CANYON

N
W   E
S

ALSO SEE MAPS
ON PAGES 86 and 105

PALISADES DRIVE

PARKER MESA
OVERLOOK
1,530'

TOPANGA
STATE PARK

TOPANGA CANYON

TOPANGA CANYON

LOS LIONES TR.

P

PASEO

PARKER CANYON

LOS LIONES CANYON

MIRAMAR

BLVD

LOS LIONES DRIVE

SUNSET BLVD

PACIFIC COAST HIGHWAY

1

TO
SANTA
MONICA

**PARKER MESA
OVERLOOK**
from PASEO MIRAMAR

*Pacific
Ocean*

Hike 48
Santa Ynez Canyon Trail
to Santa Ynez Waterfall
TOPANGA STATE PARK

Hiking distance: 3 miles round trip
Hiking time: 1.5 hours
Elevation gain: 300 feet
Maps: U.S.G.S. Topanga
       Santa Monica Mountains East Trail Map

Summary of hike: Santa Ynez Canyon is lush stream-fed canyon and natural sanctuary filled with oaks, willows, sycamores, and bay laurels. The trail follows a forested canyon bottom with numerous stream crossings. Santa Ynez Waterfall drops off the cliffs at the end of a narrow, steep-walled branch of the main canyon. The 18-foot cataract resides in a peaceful grotto surrounded by sandstone cliffs and fern-lined pools.

Driving directions: From Santa Monica, drive 3 miles northbound on the Pacific Coast Highway/Highway 1 to Sunset Boulevard. Turn right and drive 0.4 miles to Palisades Drive. Turn left and continue 2.4 miles to Vereda de la Montura. Turn left and park at the end of the road 0.1 mile ahead.

Hiking directions: Pass the trailhead gate and descend steps to the creek. Follow the east bank of the creek under the shade of sycamore and oak trees. Cross stepping stones over a side stream and continue up canyon. Cross the creek four consecutive times. After a huge sculpted sandstone outcrop is a trail split at Quarry Canyon. Stay to the left and cross to the west side of the creek and a posted trail split at a half mile. The left fork leads 1.5 miles to Trippet Ranch (Hikes 44—46). Bear right on the Waterfall Trail, and cross to the east side of the creek. Follow the watercourse, crossing four more times as the steep-walled canyon tightly narrows. Work your way up the canyon, passing a jumble of boulders and sandstone formations with caves. Boulder-hop up the fern-lined rock grotto to the waterfall at the end of the box canyon. Just before reaching the falls, a path on the right climbs the east canyon wall to an overlook of the canyon.

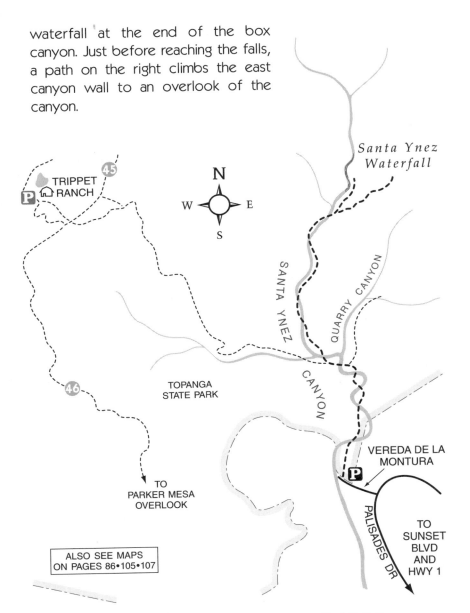

SANTA YNEZ CANYON
SANTA YNEZ WATERFALL
TOPANGA STATE PARK

Hike 49
Temescal Canyon Loop
TOPANGA STATE PARK

Hiking distance: 4.2 mile loop
Hiking time: 2 hours
Elevation gain: 1,000 feet
Maps: U.S.G.S. Topanga
Santa Monica Mountains East Trail Map

Summary of hike: Temescal Canyon is a creek-fed canyon within Topanga State Park that is shaded by oaks, maples, and sycamores. This loop hike climbs the hillside cliffs on the west side of the canyon to spectacular views of Los Angeles and the Pacific Ocean. The return route drops into the tree-shaded canyon to a footbridge at the seasonal Temescal Canyon Falls, framed by huge volcanic rocks. The trail begins at Temescal Gateway Park in Pacific Palisades.

Driving directions: From Santa Monica, drive 2 miles northbound on the Pacific Coast Highway/Highway 1 to Temescal Canyon Road. Turn right and drive 1.3 miles to the end of Temescal Canyon Road, crossing Sunset Boulevard en route. Park in the Temescal Gateway parking lot at the conference and retreat center. A parking fee is required.

Hiking directions: Walk to the top of the road, and follow the trail signs on the left to a posted junction. The Waterfall Trail to the right is our return route. Begin the loop to the left on the Temescal Ridge Trail. Zigzag up the west canyon wall, entering Topanga State Park at 0.3 miles. Short switchbacks continue uphill to the open ridge, with sweeping views of Santa Ynez Canyon, Pacific Palisades, Santa Monica, and the entire Santa Monica Bay. Continue up the ridge overlooking Temescal Canyon to a posted 4-way junction at 1.8 miles. The left fork leads 1 mile to Bienveneda Avenue in Pacific Palisades. The right fork descends into the canyon, our return route. Continue straight ahead, climbing a half mile to wind-sculpted Skull Rock.

After viewing the carved sandstone formation, return to the 4-way junction. Take the Temescal Canyon Trail to the left and steeply descend into the canyon, passing the Trailer Canyon Trail on the left. At the canyon floor is a wooden footbridge over the creek in a rock grotto just below Temescal Canyon Falls. The trail parallels the creek downstream on the east canyon wall. At the canyon floor, wind through the parklands under groves of eucalyptus, sycamore, and coastal oak, back to the trailhead.

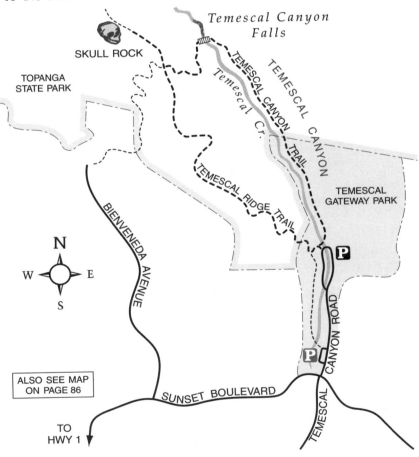

TEMESCAL CANYON
TOPANGA STATE PARK

Hike 50
Inspiration Point Loop Trail
WILL ROGERS STATE HISTORIC PARK
Open 8 a.m. to 5 p.m. daily

Hiking distance: 2 mile loop
Hiking time: 1 hour
Elevation gain: 300 feet
Maps: U.S.G.S. Topanga
Santa Monica Mountains East Trail Map
Will Rogers State Historic Park Trail map

Summary of hike: Will Rogers State Historic Park is a 186-acre retreat in the hills above Santa Monica. At the upper reaches of the park is Inspiration Point, a broad, flat knoll overlooking the beautiful park grounds and the rugged mountain canyons and ridges. The expansive views extend from downtown Los Angeles to Santa Monica and across Santa Monica Bay to Palos Verdes. Inspiration Point Loop Trail, designed by Rogers himself, is a two-mile trail that climbs the undeveloped hillside behind the ranch to Inspiration Point. The top of the loop connects with the eastern terminus of the Backbone Trail, which crosses the spine of the Santa Monica Mountains for 64 miles to Point Mugu State Park. Picnic grounds, horse riding stables, and daily tours of Will Rogers' 31-room ranch home make visiting this state park a great way to spend the day. For a longer hike, continue with Hike 51.

Driving directions: From Santa Monica, drive 1.6 miles northbound on the Pacific Coast Highway/Highway 1 to Chautauqua Boulevard. Turn right and continue 0.9 miles to Sunset Boulevard. Turn right again. Drive 0.5 miles and turn left at Will Rogers State Park Road. The parking area is 0.7 miles ahead at the end of the road. A parking fee is required.

Hiking directions: Begin the hike from Will Rogers' home, built in 1928, and the visitor center. Head west (left) past the tennis courts to a fire road—the Inspiration Point Loop Trail.

Take the fire road to the right and climb the ridge, heading north above Rivas Canyon. Climb steadily, reaching the Inspiration Point junction at 0.8 miles near the top of the knoll. Bear right to the overlook on the flat knoll. After resting and savoring the views of the entire ranch, return to the main loop. Continue north past the Backbone Trail by an information kiosk. The main loop continues northeast and descends to the south, over-looking the polo grounds. Walk through a eucalyptus-shaded lane, returning to the well-kept park grounds and visitor center.

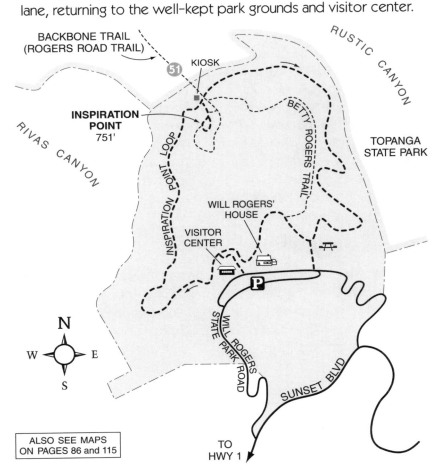

INSPIRATION POINT
WILL ROGERS STATE HISTORIC PARK

Hike 51
Rustic Canyon Loop

Hiking distance: 5 miles round trip
Hiking time: 3 hours
Elevation gain: 1,000 feet
Maps: U.S.G.S. Topanga
　　　　　Santa Monica Mountains East Trail Map

Summary of hike: Rustic Canyon is a lush stream-fed canyon on the east side of Will Rogers State Historic Park. The narrow, steep-walled canyon has a few old abandoned structures from Anatol Josepho's ranch, a friend of Will Rogers. The hike begins in the state park on the Inspiration Point Loop Trail (Hike 50). The loop trail connects with Rogers Road Trail, the easternmost segment of the Backbone Trail, designed by both Rogers and Josepho. The trail straddles the razor-point ridge between Rustic and Rivas Canyons (back cover photo). The canyon and ocean views are spectacular. The hike returns to the state park along the floor of secluded Rustic Canyon, following the year-round watercourse of Rustic Creek.

Driving directions: Same as Hike 50.

Hiking directions: Follow the hiking directions for Hike 50 for one mile to the Backbone Trail at the information kiosk. Leave the Inspiration Point Loop Trail, and take the Rogers Road Trail (Backbone Trail). Climb north on the narrow ridge between Rustic Canyon and Rivas Canyon. At 1.5 miles, cross Chicken Ridge Bridge (back cover photo), and follow the steep knife-edged slope. At just under 2 miles is a junction on a saddle. Leave the Backbone Trail and steeply descend into Rustic Canyon on the right, dropping nearly 700 feet in a half mile. At the canyon floor, cross Rustic Creek to the Rustic Canyon Trail and an old barn from the Josepho Ranch. The left fork heads up canyon and connects with Camp Josepho, a Boy Scout camp, and the Sullivan Ridge Fire Road (Hike 52). For this hike, bear right and head south, crisscrossing Rustic Creek downstream through a forest of sycamore, walnut, cottonwood, and thick pockets of poison oak. Weave through the canyon bottom past abandoned structures and a small dam. The vertical rock-walled canyon narrows, then widens out. The path leaves the canyon and returns to the polo field across from Will Rogers' home.

TO CAMP JOSEPHO

OLD BARN

RUSTIC

Rustic

RUSTIC CANYON

BACKBONE TRAIL

RIVAS CANYON

CHICKEN RIDGE BRIDGE

(ROGERS ROAD TRAIL)

Creek

TOPANGA STATE PARK

KIOSK

INSPIRATION POINT

INSPIRATION POINT LOOP

50

N
W E
S

VISITOR CENTER

P

WILL ROGERS STATE PARK

WILL ROGERS STATE PARK ROAD

SUNSET BLVD

ALSO SEE MAPS ON PAGES 86 and 113

TO HWY 1

RUSTIC CANYON LOOP

Hike 52
Sullivan Canyon

Hiking distance: 8.6 miles round trip
Hiking time: 4 hours
Elevation gain: 1,200 feet
Maps: U.S.G.S. Topanga
Santa Monica Mountains East Trail Map

Summary of hike: Sullivan Canyon is a secluded steam-fed canyon with huge stands of sycamore, oak, willow, and walnut trees. The trail follows the intermittent stream through the steep-walled canyon beneath a rich canopy of green foliage. After meandering up the long, pristine canyon, the trail climbs the chaparral-covered slopes to Sullivan Ridge and magnificent canyon views. This hike can be combined with Hike 53 for a 10-mile loop.

Driving directions: From Santa Monica, drive 1.6 miles northbound on the Pacific Coast Highway/Highway 1 to Chautauqua Boulevard and turn right. Continue 0.9 miles to Sunset Boulevard and turn right. Drive 2.8 miles and turn left on Mandeville Canyon Road. Turn left again at the first street—Westridge Road—and drive 1.2 miles to Bayliss Road. Turn left on Bayliss Road, and go 0.3 miles to Queensferry Road. Turn left and park near the trailhead gate.

Hiking directions: Step around the vehicle-restricting gate. Walk 0.2 miles down the paved service road to the floor of Sullivan Canyon. Head right, up the serene canyon floor under a lush forest canopy. At 1 mile, cross a seasonal stream and pass sandstone outcroppings. At 3.5 miles, Sullivan Canyon curves right (northeast). The trail curves left (northwest) up a narrow side canyon. Climb the west canyon wall overlooking Sullivan Canyon. Follow the contours of the mountain up to the ridge and a T-junction with the Sullivan Ridge Fire Road at 4.3 miles. This is our turnaround spot. To hike a 10-mile loop, bear right up to Mulholland Drive and continue with Hike 53.

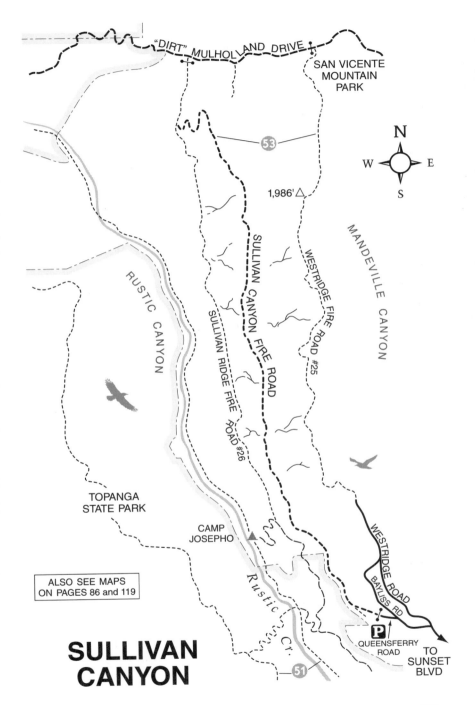

"DIRT" MULHOLLAND DRIVE

SAN VICENTE
MOUNTAIN
PARK

53

1,986'△

N
W E
S

RUSTIC CANYON

SULLIVAN CANYON FIRE ROAD

SULLIVAN RIDGE FIRE ROAD #26

WESTRIDGE FIRE ROAD #25

MANDEVILLE CANYON

TOPANGA
STATE PARK

CAMP
JOSEPHO

Rustic Cr.

51

ALSO SEE MAPS
ON PAGES 86 and 119

WESTRIDGE ROAD

BAYLISS RD

P
QUEENSFERRY
ROAD

TO
SUNSET
BLVD

SULLIVAN
CANYON

Hike 53
Sullivan Canyon—Westridge Fire Road Loop

Hiking distance: 10 mile loop
Hiking time: 5 hours
Elevation gain: 1,300 feet
Maps: U.S.G.S. Topanga and Conoga Park
Santa Monica Mountains East Trail Map

Summary of hike: This loop hike follows the forested canyon floor of Sullivan Canyon and climbs the chaparral covered slopes to Sullivan Ridge. The trail follows "Dirt" Mulholland, an unimproved road along the ridge overlooking the west end of Los Angeles, the San Fernando Valley, and the Encino Reservoir. Return from San Vicente Mountain Park, formerly the NIKE Missile Control Site, an old military outpost active from 1956 through 1968. (The 10-acre park is now a self-guided interpretive center that describes its former life.) The trail descends on the Westridge Fire Road, a hiking and biking route straddling the ridgeline between Sullivan and Mandeville Canyons.

Driving directions: Same as Hike 52.

Hiking directions: Follow the hiking directions for Hike 52 to the T-junction with the Sullivan Ridge Fire Road. Bear right and head north on the ridge between Rustic Canyon and Sullivan Canyon, reaching Mulholland Drive at a half mile. Walk around the gate and follow Mulholland Drive to the right for 0.8 miles, overlooking the Encino Reservoir and the San Fernando Valley. Pass another gate and bear right into San Vicente Mountain Park, the defunct missile silo site. Walk up the paved road and through the park, passing picnic areas and vista overlooks. Take the Westridge Fire Road (also known as Sullivan Ridge East) along the narrow ridge dividing Sullivan and Mandeville Canyons. Follow the ridge south to the high point of the hike at 1,986 feet. Gradually descend along the contours of the ridge, overlooking Sullivan Canyon, Rustic Canyon, the west ridge of Temescal Canyon, and the Los Angeles basin. The fire road exits at Westridge Road. Walk a half mile down Westridge Road, and turn right on Bayliss Road. Walk another half mile to Queensferry Road and turn right, returning to the trailhead.

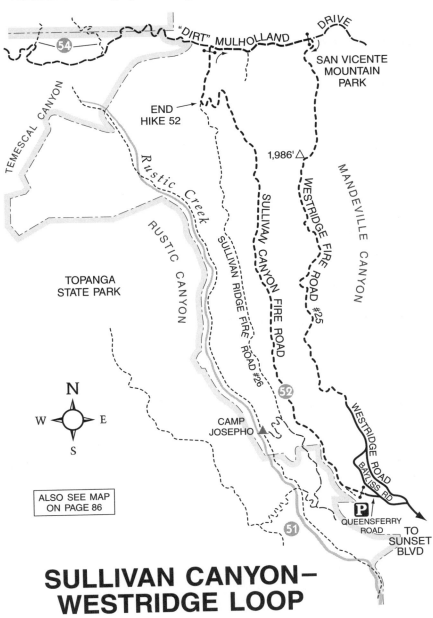

SULLIVAN CANYON—
WESTRIDGE LOOP

Hike 54
Caballero Canyon Loop
MARVIN BRAUDE MULHOLLAND GATEWAY PARK

Hiking distance: 3.7 mile loop
Hiking time: 2 hours
Elevation gain: 600 feet
Maps: U.S.G.S. Conoga Park
Santa Monica Mountains East Trail Map

Summary of hike: Caballero Canyon, on the north border of Topanga State Park, offers easy access to a network of hiking and biking trails. The trailhead is in Marvin Braude Mulholland Gateway Park, a grassy hillside park with picnic sites in the San Fernando Valley near Tarzana. From the north slope of the Santa Monica Mountains, the trail connects with an unpaved section of Mulholland Drive. This hike follows the ridge and returns down Caballero Canyon through sycamore and willow groves.

Driving directions: From the Ventura Freeway/Highway 101 in Tarzana, exit on Reseda Boulevard. Drive 3.4 miles south into Marvin Braude Mulholland Gateway Park, and park at the end of the road.

Hiking directions: From the south end of Reseda Boulevard, take the gated, unpaved fire road up the hill into Topanga State Park. Pass a second vehicle gate to "Dirt" Mulholland at 0.2 miles. Bear left on the wide road, and follow the ridge across the head of Caballero Canyon, curving south then east. From the ridge are southern views into Temescal and Rustic Canyons and northern views into Caballero Canyon. At 0.7 miles, pass the Bent Arrow Trail, a connector trail to Temescal Ridge Fire Road, and continue along the ridge. Just before the road curves left around a prominent hill known as Farmer Ridge, watch for the Caballero Canyon Trail on the left. Bear left and descend down the east flank of the canyon. Wind downhill to the canyon floor dotted with sycamore trees. Head north, parallel to an inter-mittent stream, and meander through the canyon to Reseda

Boulevard at the old Caballero Canyon trailhead. Bear left and follow landscaped Reseda Boulevard above Caballero Canyon for 1.2 miles, back to the trailhead.

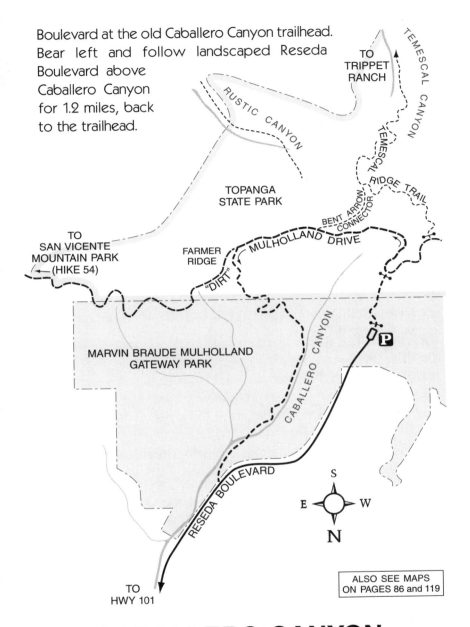

ALSO SEE MAPS
ON PAGES 86 and 119

CABALLERO CANYON
MARVIN BRAUDE MULHOLLAND
GATEWAY PARK

Hike 55
Getty View Trail

Hiking distance: 3.6 miles round trip
Hiking time: 2 hours
Elevation gain: 600 feet
Maps: U.S.G.S. Beverly Hills
       Santa Monica Mountains Conservancy map

Summary of hike: The Getty View Trail in Bel Air ascends the steep hillside from Sepulveda Pass to Casiano Fire Road, an unpaved road on the ridgeline. A three-quarter mile climb through chaparral and pockets of live oak and toyon provides access to a section of the 376-acre Sepulveda Pass Open Space. The ridge-top trail overlooks Hoag Canyon, with sweeping vistas of the Getty Center Museum, West Los Angeles, Santa Monica, and the Pacific Ocean.

Driving directions: Heading northbound from Los Angeles on the San Diego Freeway/Interstate 405, take the Getty Center Drive exit. Turn left (north) 0.1 mile to the trailhead parking lot on the right, just before crossing under the freeway.

Heading southbound from the San Fernando Valley on the San Diego Freeway/Interstate 405, take the Getty Center Drive exit. Turn left (south) and cross under the freeway to the trailhead parking lot, immediately on the left.

Hiking directions: From the trailhead map, bear left (north) on the signed trail, and head up the side canyon past sycamore trees. Switchbacks lead up the chaparral covered hillside east of Sepulveda Pass. The views improve with every step. Switchbacks make the elevation gain very easy. At 0.6 miles, the trail reaches the ridge and a T-junction with the Casiano Fire Road. Bear left on the ridge-hugging dirt road above the deep and undeveloped Hoag Canyon. A footpath parallels the road on the west, gaining elevation to an incredible overlook by an isolated oak tree. The footpath parallels the cliffs and rejoins the fire road. A short distance ahead, a second side path on the left parallels the road to additional overlooks before rejoining the road again. At 0.4 miles, the pavement begins at a gated community. Return south, back to the Getty View Trail junction. Continue south on the fire road while descending along the ridge. An undulating footpath parallels the east side of the road overlooking Hoag Canyon. At 0.7 miles the fire road ends at Casiano Road in Bel Air Estates, where views open up across West Los Angeles. Return along the same route.

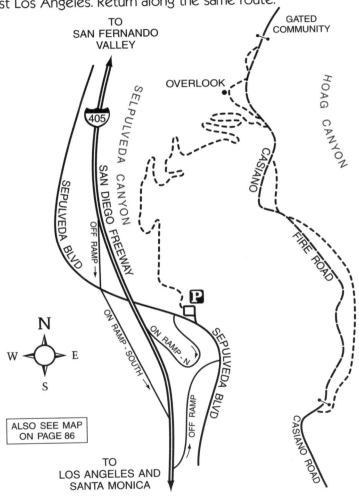

GETTY VIEW TRAIL

Hike 56
Hastian—Discovery Loop
LOWER FRANKLIN CANYON PARK

Hiking distance: 3 mile loop
Hiking time: 1.5 hours
Elevation gain: 400 feet
Maps: U.S.G.S. Beverly Hills
       Franklin Canyon Park Nature Trails map

Summary of hike: The Hastian—Discovery Loop, in Lower Franklin Canyon Park, winds through the 105-acre Franklin Canyon Ranch site. The ranch is nestled in a deep valley in the mountains above Beverly Hills. These loop trails climb through the canyon bottom woodlands to the chaparral covered slopes. The Hastian Trail climbs the east wall of Franklin Canyon on a fire road to spectacular vistas of the lower canyon, Franklin Canyon Reservoir, West Los Angeles, and the Pacific Ocean. The Discovery Trail follows the canyon floor through groves of sycamore, oak, and black walnut trees.

Driving directions: From Sunset Boulevard in Beverly Hills, head north on Beverly Drive for 0.6 miles. At the fork, go left on Beverly Drive, where the main road continues as Coldwater Canyon Drive. Continue 0.8 miles and curve right onto Franklin Canyon Drive. Drive 1.1 mile to Lake Drive. Turn right and drive 0.3 miles to the posted trailhead parking area on the left.
From the Ventura Freeway/Highway 101 in Studio City, exit on Coldwater Canyon Drive. Head 2.5 miles south to the intersection with Mulholland Drive by the Coldwater Canyon Park/TreePeople Park. Make a 90-degree right turn onto Franklin Canyon Drive. Continue 1.4 miles to Lake Drive. Curve left onto Lake Drive, and go 0.3 miles to the posted trailhead parking area on the left.

Hiking directions: Take the posted Hastian Trail, a fire road, past the trail gate. Traverse the hillside high above Lake Drive. The easy, uphill grade climbs the east canyon wall. The trail curves left and makes a wide sweeping loop around a side canyon, steadily gaining elevation to an overlook of Lower Franklin Canyon, Westwood, Santa Monica, and the ocean. The main trail curves left and continues up to the ridge, leaving Franklin Canyon and the park. Take the narrow footpath on the right by the wood pole and wind down the hill. The serpentine path exits the hillside at 2.3 miles on a broad grassy lawn by the old Doheny house, a Spanish-style stucco house built in 1935. Cross Lake Road to the Discovery Trail. Curve right and head north, parallel to the park road along the lower west canyon slope. The trail joins Lake Drive 50 yards south of the trailhead. Return to the left.

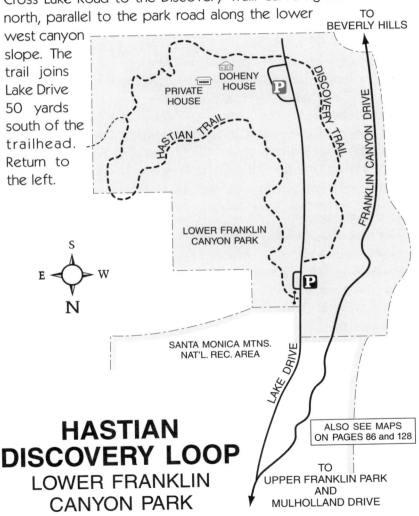

TO
BEVERLY HILLS

DOHENY HOUSE

PRIVATE HOUSE

P

DISCOVERY TRAIL

HASTIAN TRAIL

FRANKLIN CANYON DRIVE

S
E
W
N

LOWER FRANKLIN CANYON PARK

P

SANTA MONICA MTNS. NAT'L. REC. AREA

LAKE DRIVE

HASTIAN DISCOVERY LOOP
LOWER FRANKLIN CANYON PARK

ALSO SEE MAPS
ON PAGES 86 and 128

TO
UPPER FRANKLIN PARK
AND
MULHOLLAND DRIVE

Hike 57
Franklin Canyon Lake • Heavenly Pond Loop
UPPER FRANKLIN CANYON PARK

Hiking distance: 1 mile loop
Hiking time: 30 minutes
Elevation gain: 30 feet
Maps: U.S.G.S. Beverly Hills
      N.P.S. Franklin Canyon Site
      Franklin Canyon Park Nature Trails map

map next page

Summary of hike: Franklin Canyon Park is a 605-acre wildlife refuge and tranquil retreat just minutes from Beverly Hills. The pastoral open space of Upper Franklin Canyon centers around Franklin Canyon Lake, a beautiful 9-acre man-made lake which is part of the California migratory bird route. The famous opening sequence of the Andy Griffith Show was filmed on the trail near the lake. This hike circles the serene lake under sycamores and oaks. To the east of the lake is Heavenly Pond. Circling the pond is the Wodoc Nature Trail, a wheelchair-accessible path through a natural riparian habitat.

Driving directions: From Sunset Boulevard in Beverly Hills, head north on Beverly Drive for 0.6 miles. At the fork, go left on Beverly Drive, where the main road continues as Coldwater Canyon Drive. Continue 0.8 miles and curve right onto Franklin Canyon Drive. Drive 1.8 miles, winding through Franklin Canyon Park, to the large William O. Douglas Outdoor Classroom and Sooky Goldman Nature Center parking lot on the right.

From the Ventura Freeway/Highway 101 in Studio City, exit on Coldwater Canyon Drive. Head 2.5 miles south to the intersection with Mulholland Drive by the Coldwater Canyon Park/TreePeople Park. Make a 90-degree right turn onto Franklin Canyon Drive. Continue 0.7 miles to the William O. Douglas Outdoor Classroom and Sooky Goldman Nature Center parking lot on the left.

Hiking directions: Follow the park road to the left (south) for 30 yards to a road on the right by the maintenance shop. Curve right and descend steps on the left to the trail. Pass the surge basin to a trail split. Both paths parallel the lake and merge at a picnic area by the park road. (The left fork skirts the edge of the lake.) Follow the road to the left 50 yards to the Wodoc Nature Trail at Heavenly Pond. Loop around the serene pond on the paved path. Back at the road, continue south above the lake, and cross the dam at the end of the lake. After crossing, descend steps on the Chernoff Trail, and follow the east banks of the lake through a shady woodland and a picnic area. At the Franklin Lake spillway, curve right to the road, and bear left 100 yards, returning to the parking area. (If the spillway is dry, you may cross over it to complete the loop and return to the right.)

Hike 58
Blinderman Trail
UPPER FRANKLIN CANYON PARK

Hiking distance: 1.5 mile loop
Hiking time: 40 minutes
Elevation gain: 200 feet
Maps: U.S.G.S. Beverly Hills and Van Nuys
N.P.S. Franklin Canyon Site
Franklin Canyon Park Nature Trails map

map
next page

Summary of hike: Upper Franklin Canyon Park is home to the Sooky Goldman Nature Center and the William O. Douglas Outdoor Classroom, providing educational programs to the public and local schools. The Blinderman Trail is adjacent to the nature center. The path traverses the canyon slopes through chaparral, strolls along stream-fed side canyons with meadows, and climbs to overlooks of Franklin Canyon Lake and the entire canyon oasis.

Driving directions: Same as Hike 57.

Hiking directions: Cross the wooden bridge to the information board. The left fork is a northbound connector trail to

Coldwater Canyon Park (Hike 59). Bear right and wind up the hill to the Sooky Goldman Nature Center. Walk through the courtyard to the back (east) side of the buildings and the posted Blinderman Trail. Twenty yards up the footpath is a trail fork. The left fork leads through walnut groves to a maintenance road. Head right and traverse the hillside, curving left to a trail split. Take the left fork and climb up the hillside to an overlook of Franklin Lake. Continue uphill to the ridge with views down the entire length of Franklin Canyon. The ridge path leads to additional observation points. Return to the main trail, and continue on the south fork to the canyon floor by Geology Rock. Bear left on the dirt road, passing Wild Pond on the right to a 4-way junction. (En route, a short side path loops around the pond to Sycamore Meadow.) Bear left and climb steps up the hillside.

The undulating path crosses a wooden bridge and returns to the canyon floor at a T-junction. The left fork leads 100 yards to a large grassy flat with towering redwoods at the park boundary. The right fork returns to the 4-way junction. Take the left fork and climb the hill through a eucalyptus grove. Curve right to the park road by Franklin Canyon Lake. Follow the road to the right, returning to the trailhead parking lot.

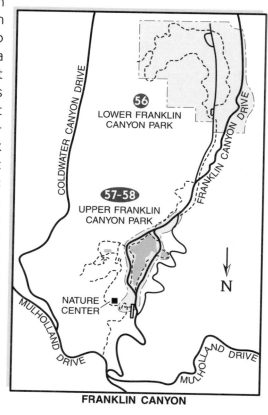

FRANKLIN CANYON

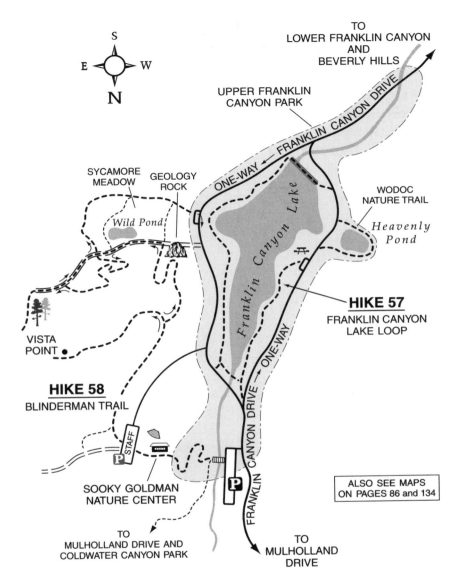

S
E · W
N

TO
LOWER FRANKLIN CANYON
AND
BEVERLY HILLS

UPPER FRANKLIN
CANYON PARK

FRANKLIN CANYON DRIVE

ONE-WAY

SYCAMORE
MEADOW

GEOLOGY
ROCK

WODOC
NATURE TRAIL

Wild Pond

Franklin Canyon Lake

Heavenly Pond

HIKE 57
FRANKLIN CANYON
LAKE LOOP

VISTA
POINT ●

ONE-WAY

FRANKLIN CANYON DRIVE →

HIKE 58
BLINDERMAN TRAIL

STAFF

P

P

SOOKY GOLDMAN
NATURE CENTER

ALSO SEE MAPS
ON PAGES 86 and 134

TO
MULHOLLAND DRIVE AND
COLDWATER CANYON PARK

TO
MULHOLLAND
DRIVE

FRANKLIN CANYON
LAKE LOOP
BLINDERMAN TRAIL
UPPER FRANKLIN CANYON PARK

Hike 59
Coldwater Canyon Park—Wilacre Park Loop

12601 Mulholland Drive

Hiking distance: 2.7 mile loop
Hiking time: 1.5 hours
Elevation gain: 500 feet
Maps: U.S.G.S. Van Nuys
       Trails Illustrated Santa Monica Mountains Nat'l. Rec. Area

map
page 134

Summary of hike: Coldwater Canyon Park (44 acres) is home to TreePeople Park, a non-profit educational facility known for planting more than a million trees. TreePeople, which maintains and improves Coldwater Canyon Park, includes a tree nursery, fruit orchard, organic garden, and the Magic Forest Nature Trail. Wilacre Park, in Studio City, is a 128-acre undeveloped greenbelt of chaparral covered ridges and wooded canyons surrounded by residential homes. This loop hike crosses Coldwater Canyon Park and Wilacre Park with panoramic views of the San Fernando Valley.

Driving directions: From Sunset Boulevard in Beverly Hills, head north on Beverly Drive for 0.6 miles. At the fork, go right onto Coldwater Canyon Drive. Continue 3 miles to an intersection with Mulholland Drive. Go to the left, staying on Coldwater Canyon Drive, and drive 0.4 miles to the posted Coldwater Canyon/TreePeople Park on the right. Turn right into the parking area.

From the Ventura Freeway/Highway 101 in Studio City, exit on Coldwater Canyon Drive. Head 2.5 miles south to the intersection with Mulholland Drive. The posted Coldwater Canyon/TreePeople Park entrance is on the left (east) side of the intersection.

Hiking directions: From the information kiosk at the far end of the parking area, bear left on the nature trail, and head 30 yards to a junction. Cut back sharply to the right, and follow the wide path on an easy downhill grade to the second hillside level. Switchback to the left and descend to the third level and a junction with the Dearing Mountain Trail. Begin the loop to the left, gaining elevation while crossing the head of Iredell Canyon. Cross a small saddle and curve around the hillside to sweeping birds-eye views of the valley. Continue on a slow but steady descent with wide curves. Along the way, the trail becomes a narrow, paved path, winding through cypress and pine tree groves. The trail ends at the Wilacre Park trailhead on Fryman Road at 1.5 miles. For a loop hike, follow Fryman Road 0.15 miles to the right to Iredell Street. Bear right and walk a half mile through a residential area, curving left onto Iredell Lane to the cul-de-sac at the end of the street. (The trail to Fryman Canyon, [Hike 60] is to the left, shortly before the cul-de-sac.) Pick up the posted trail, and ascend the hillside along the open space boundary. Make a wide right curve, completing the loop. Return to the left and stroll through the Magic Forest Nature Trail.

Hike 60
Dearing Mountain Trail
Fryman Canyon Park to TreePeople Park

Hiking distance: 5 miles round trip
Hiking time: 2.5 hours
Elevation gain: 500 feet
Maps: U.S.G.S. Beverly Hills and Van Nuys
       Trails Illustrated Santa Monica Mountains Nat'l. Rec. Area

map
page 134

Summary of hike: Fryman Canyon Park, encompassing more than 120 acres, sits on a north-facing hillside bordering Mulholland Drive. At the trailhead, the Nancy Hoover Pohl Overlook (formerly known as the Fryman Canyon Overlook) provides views across the wooded canyon to the San Fernando Valley, Santa Susana Mountains, and the San Gabriel Mountains. The Dearing Mountain Trail (also known as the Betty B. Dearing Trail) descends into the canyon, connecting Fryman Canyon Park with Coldwater Canyon Park and Wilacre Park.

Driving directions: From Sunset Boulevard in Beverly Hills, head north on Beverly Drive for 0.6 miles. At the fork, go right onto Coldwater Canyon Drive. Continue 3 miles to an intersection with Mulholland Drive. Turn right on Mulholland Drive, and go 2 miles to the posted Fryman Canyon Park entrance on the left. Turn left into the parking lot.

From the Ventura Freeway/Highway 101 in Studio City, exit on Laurel Canyon Boulevard. Head 2.8 miles south to the intersection with Mulholland Drive. Turn right on Mulholland Drive, and drive 0.8 miles to the posted Fryman Canyon Park entrance on the right.

Hiking directions: To the left of the trailhead, steps lead up to the Pohl (Fryman Canyon) Overlook. The posted Dearing Mountain Trail descends to a junction a short distance ahead. Bear left and zigzag down seven switchbacks into Fryman Canyon. Follow the contours of the hillside, and make a horseshoe right bend across a spring-fed drainage. Pass remnants of a few old cars, and continue on the canyon wall to a T-junction. Take the left fork and stroll through a mature grove of oak and eucalyptus trees. Cross a stream in a ravine and bear left. Cross another drainage by a huge sandstone outcrop, and pass an overlook of a few showcase homes. Curve right on a footpath and traverse the sloping hillside. Descend steps and emerge on Iredell Lane at 2 miles. Bear left 0.1 mile to the cul-de-sac. Pick up the posted trail, and ascend the hillside for a half mile to a junction. Bear left and stroll through the Magic Forest Nature Trail, or ascend the steps to the park headquarters and an educational facility at TreePeople Park. Return by retracing your steps.

Hike 61
Fryman Canyon Loop

Hiking distance: 4 mile loop
Hiking time: 2 hours
Elevation gain: 500 feet
Maps: U.S.G.S. Beverly Hills and Van Nuys
  Trails Illustrated Santa Monica Mountains Nat'l. Rec. Area

map
next page

Summary of hike: This hike passes through Fryman Canyon Park and a quiet residential area that borders the park, turning Hike 60 into a loop hike. Fryman Canyon Park, Coldwater Canyon Park (Hike 59), Wilacre Park (Hike 59), and Franklin Canyon Park (Hikes 56—58) are collectively referred to as Cross Mountain Park. The mountain paths through this 1,000-acre park system cross ridges, wind through chaparral covered hillsides, and meander up stream-fed canyons.

Driving directions: Same as Hike 60.

Hiking directions: To the left of the trailhead, steps lead up to the Pohl (Fryman Canyon) Overlook. The posted Dearing Mountain Trail gradually descends on the chaparral covered slope. A short distance ahead is a junction on the left, our return route. Stay straight, following the contours of the hillside on a near-level grade that overlooks Fryman Canyon. Pass oak groves to a trail split at 0.4 miles. The right (upper trail) dead-ends in a quarter mile near Laurel Canyon Boulevard. Take the lower (left) fork, dropping down into the canyon to a T-junction with an unpaved road behind a row of homes fronted on Briarcliff Lane. Follow the road downhill to the left for 0.3 miles along the park boundary to the base of Fryman Canyon, where the road becomes paved. Detour left for 100 yards up the canyon on the footpath. Cross a ravine and meander up the canyon floor on the tree-shaded path. Curving right is a narrow, stream-fed canyon where the trail fades and becomes hard to follow. Return to the road. Bear left 0.1 mile to the south end of Fryman Road. Follow Fryman Road to the left 0.4 miles to Iredell Street. Bear left and walk up the residential road, curving left on Iredell Lane. One hundred yards before the cul-de-sac, pick up the Dearing Mountain Trail on the left. Climb the steps and wind through Fryman Canyon under the shade of eucalyptus and oak groves. Cross a spring-fed drainage, and steadily climb seven switchbacks to the head of Fryman Canyon, completing the loop at the T-junction. Return to the trailhead on the right.

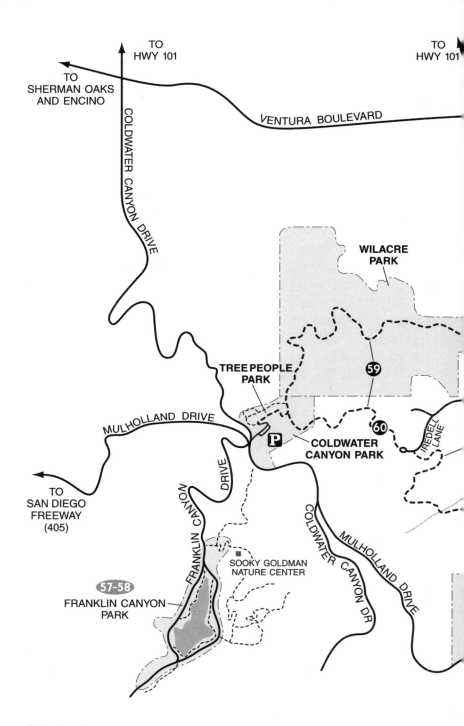

TO
HWY 101

TO
HWY 101

TO
SHERMAN OAKS
AND ENCINO

COLDWATER CANYON DRIVE

VENTURA BOULEVARD

WILACRE
PARK

TREE PEOPLE
PARK

59

60

IREDELL LANE

MULHOLLAND DRIVE

P

COLDWATER
CANYON PARK

FRANKLIN CANYON DRIVE

TO
SAN DIEGO
FREEWAY
(405)

COLDWATER CANYON DR

MULHOLLAND DRIVE

SOOKY GOLDMAN
NATURE CENTER

57-58

FRANKLIN CANYON
PARK

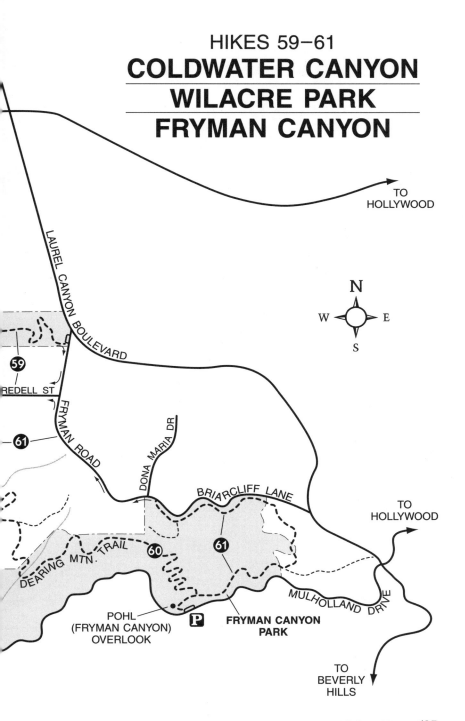

TO
HOLLYWOOD

N
W ◆ E
S

LAUREL CANYON BOULEVARD

59

REDELL ST

FRYMAN ROAD

61

DONA MARIA DR

BRIARCLIFF LANE

TO
HOLLYWOOD

DEARING MTN. TRAIL

60

61

MULHOLLAND DRIVE

POHL
(FRYMAN CANYON)
OVERLOOK

P

**FRYMAN CANYON
PARK**

TO
BEVERLY
HILLS

HOLLYWOOD HILLS
AND
GRIFFITH PARK

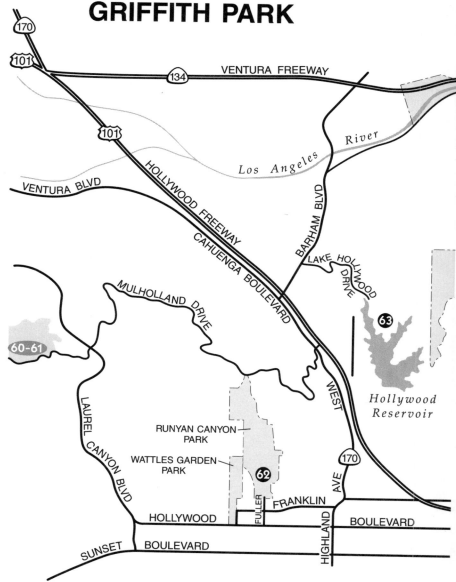

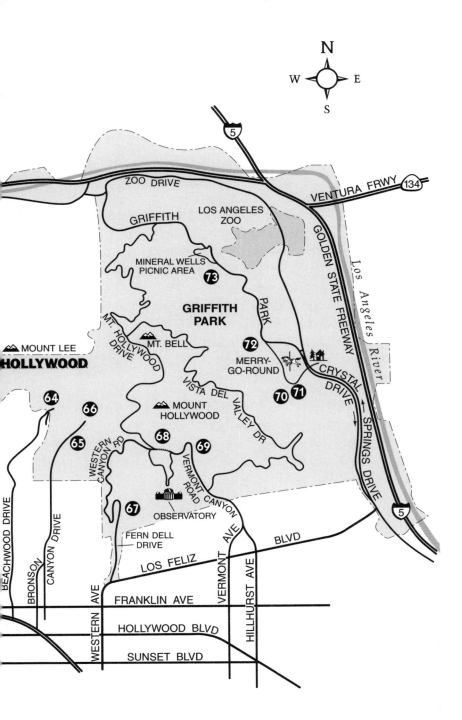

Hike 62
Runyan Canyon Park

Hiking distance: 2 mile loop
Hiking time: 1 hour
Elevation gain: 500 feet
Maps: U.S.G.S. Hollywood
Trails Illustrated Santa Monica Mountains Nat'l. Rec. Area

Summary of hike: Runyan Canyon Park, a wildlife preserve minutes from the heart of Hollywood, was purchased by the Santa Monica Mountains Conservancy and the City of Los Angeles in 1984. This trail loops around the chaparral clad hillsides of Runyan Canyon and crosses a broad gorge overlooking the urban canyon wilderness and Hollywood. The loop trail passes the ruins of a pool house designed by Frank Lloyd Wright and lived in for several years by Errol Flynn. Remnants of the old stone foundation and the exotic landscaping are all that remain of the ruined oasis. Runyan Canyon is a popular dog walking park.

Driving directions: At the intersection of Franklin Avenue and Highland Avenue in Hollywood, drive 0.3 miles west on Franklin to Fuller Avenue. Turn right and continue 0.5 miles to The Pines gate at the end of the road. Park along the street where a space is available.

Hiking directions: Walk through The Pines entrance gate into Runyan Canyon Park at the end of Fuller Avenue. A short distance past the entrance is a trail to the left—the beginning of the loop. Take this trail as it curves along the chaparral covered hillside parallel to the canyon floor. At one mile, near the head of Runyan Canyon, the trail circles over to the east side of the canyon. Watch for a narrow trail to the right heading back towards the south. This trail leads to Cloud's Rest, an exceptional overlook with 360-degree panoramic views. The trail continues to Inspiration Point and the Wright pool house ruins, then descends to the canyon floor and back to the trailhead.

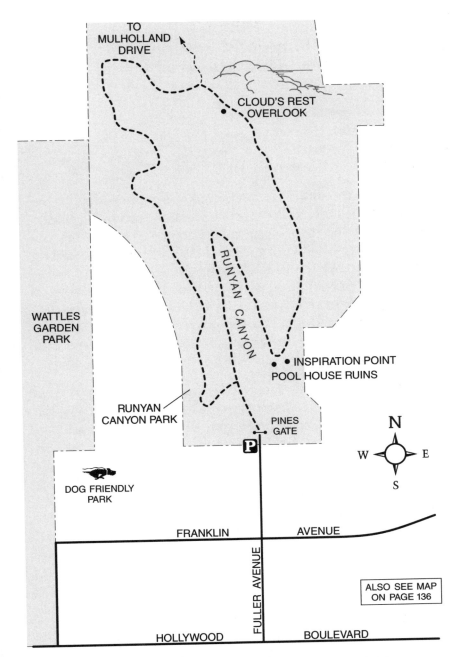

TO MULHOLLAND DRIVE

CLOUD'S REST OVERLOOK

RUNYAN CANYON

WATTLES GARDEN PARK

RUNYAN CANYON PARK

INSPIRATION POINT
POOL HOUSE RUINS

PINES GATE

P

N
W   E
S

DOG FRIENDLY PARK

FRANKLIN   AVENUE

FULLER AVENUE

ALSO SEE MAP
ON PAGE 136

HOLLYWOOD   BOULEVARD

RUNYAN CANYON PARK

Hike 63
Hollywood Reservoir

Open weekdays 6:30 to 10 a.m. and 2 to 5 p.m.
Open weekends 6:30 a.m. to 5 p.m.

Hiking distance: 4 mile loop
Hiking time: 1.5 hours
Elevation gain: Level
Maps: U.S.G.S. Hollywood and Burbank

Summary of hike: This hike follows the perimeter of the Hollywood Reservoir on an asphalt service road that is closed to vehicles. The road, which is landscaped on both sides, is a rural retreat inside the city that is frequently used as a walking and jogging trail. The lake is fenced, preventing access to the shoreline. The tall foliage along the trail obscures full views of the reservoir except when crossing Mulholland Dam. The dam crossing is magnificent. To the north is Mount Lee and the "Hollywood" sign overlooking the beautiful reservoir below. To the south is a view of Hollywood and the Los Angeles Basin.

Driving directions: From Hollywood, take Highland Avenue north past the Hollywood Bowl, curving left onto Cahuenga Boulevard West. Continue one mile to Barham Boulevard. Turn right and cross over the Hollywood Freeway. Drive 0.2 miles to Lake Hollywood Drive and turn right. Follow the winding Lake Hollywood Drive through a residential neighborhood for 0.8 miles to the Hollywood Reservoir entrance gate on the right. Park alongside the road.

From the Hollywood Freeway/Highway 101, take the Barham Boulevard Exit, and head north 0.2 miles to Lake Hollywood Drive. Turn right and drive 0.8 miles to the Hollywood Reservoir entrance gate on the right.

Hiking directions: The reservoir entrance is on the right (south). The paved path follows the perimeter of the reservoir through the shaded evergreen forest. At the south end of the reservoir, cross Mulholland Dam. The path then loops north to

Tahoe Drive. Bear left along the
road, returning to the
parking area.

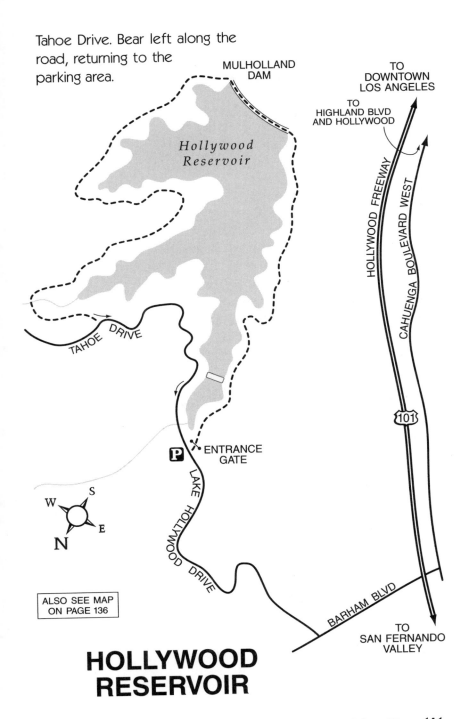

MULHOLLAND
DAM

TO
DOWNTOWN
LOS ANGELES

TO
HIGHLAND BLVD
AND HOLLYWOOD

*Hollywood
Reservoir*

HOLLYWOOD FREEWAY

CAHUENGA BOULEVARD WEST

101

TAHOE DRIVE

P ENTRANCE
    GATE

LAKE HOLLYWOOD DRIVE

W   S
   N   E

ALSO SEE MAP
ON PAGE 136

BARHAM BLVD

TO
SAN FERNANDO
VALLEY

HOLLYWOOD
RESERVOIR

Hike 64
Mount Lee and the "Hollywood" sign
GRIFFITH PARK

Hiking distance: 3 miles round trip
Hiking time: 1.5 hours
Elevation gain: 550 feet
Maps: U.S.G.S. Hollywood and Burbank

Summary of hike: This trail leads to the famous "HOLLY-WOOD" sign on the south slope of Mount Lee. The historic Los Angeles landmark was originally built in the 1920s to read "HOLLYWOODLAND," promoting real estate development in Beachwood Canyon. In 1978, entertainment celebrities donated money to replace the original sign, which was worn from time, weather, and vandalism. The sign now measures 50 feet high by 450 feet long. It sits just below the Mount Lee summit. The sign itself is fenced off from direct visitation, but the views from atop Mount Lee are superb.

Driving directions: At the intersection of Franklin Avenue and Western Avenue in Hollywood, drive 0.7 miles west on Franklin Avenue to Beachwood Drive. Turn right (north) and continue 1.7 miles up Beachwood Drive to Hollyridge Drive. Park near this intersection.

Hiking directions: From the intersection, hike up Hollyridge Drive 200 feet to the trailhead on the left. From the Hollyridge Trail, the "HOLLYWOOD" sign looms over the landscape. Follow the ridge northeast, overlooking the Sunset Horse Ranch on the left. Continue 0.5 miles to an intersection with the unmarked Mulholland Trail. Take a sharp left up this trail as it heads west on a fire road to Mount Lee Drive 0.3 miles ahead. At Mount Lee Drive, the left fork leads downhill to excellent frontal views of the sign. The right fork heads uphill to the ridge above and behind the sign, overlooking Burbank and the San Fernando Valley. Return along the same path.

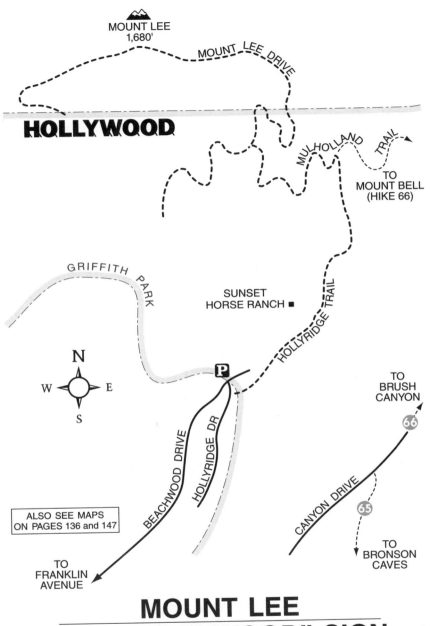

MOUNT LEE
1,680'

MOUNT LEE DRIVE

HOLLYWOOD

MULHOLLAND TRAIL

TO
MOUNT BELL
(HIKE 66)

GRIFFITH PARK

SUNSET
HORSE RANCH ■

HOLLYRIDGE TRAIL

N
W E
S

P

TO
BRUSH
CANYON

66

BEACHWOOD DRIVE

HOLLYRIDGE DR

CANYON DRIVE

65

ALSO SEE MAPS
ON PAGES 136 and 147

TO
BRONSON
CAVES

TO
FRANKLIN
AVENUE

MOUNT LEE
THE "HOLLYWOOD" SIGN
GRIFFITH PARK

Hike 65
Bronson Caves
GRIFFITH PARK

Hiking distance: 0.6 miles round trip
Hiking time: 0.5 hours
Elevation gain: 40 feet
Maps: U.S.G.S. Hollywood
Hileman's Recreational & Geological Map of Griffith Park

Summary of hike: At the southwest corner of Griffith Park is an enjoyable, short hike to one of Hollywood's most frequently filmed caves. Originally a quarry, the crushed rock from the caves was used to pave the streets of a growing Hollywood. Many western and science fiction movie producers have shot on location at these man-made caves. *Star Trek, Mission Impossible, Gunsmoke, Bonanza,* and the *Batman and Robin* series have been filmed here.

Driving directions: At the intersection of Hollywood Boulevard and Western Avenue in Hollywood, drive 0.5 miles west on Hollywood Boulevard to Bronson Avenue. Turn right and continue 1.5 miles on Bronson Avenue (which merges with Canyon Drive) past Bronson Park to the end of the road. Park in the lot on the left.

Hiking directions: From the parking lot, hike back along the park road 100 feet to the trailhead on the left (east) side of the road. The trail gently climbs a quarter mile to the caves. From here you may walk through the caves and around the hill. Return along the same path.

To extend the hike, Brush Canyon (Hike 66) heads up the road past the vehicle gate.

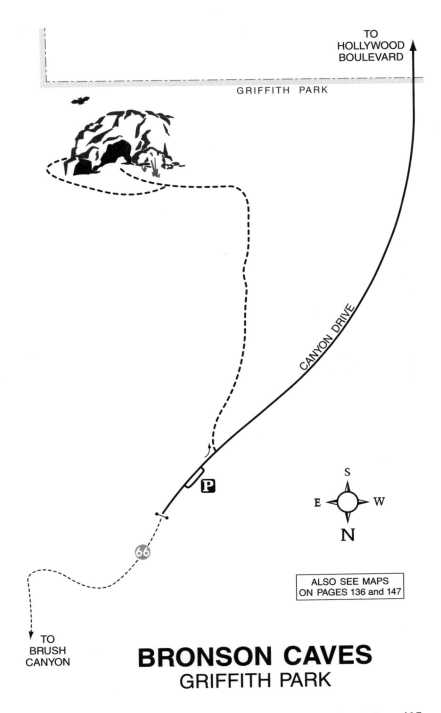

TO
HOLLYWOOD
BOULEVARD

GRIFFITH PARK

CANYON DRIVE

P

S

E ◇ W

N

ALSO SEE MAPS
ON PAGES 136 and 147

66

TO
BRUSH
CANYON

BRONSON CAVES
GRIFFITH PARK

Hike 66
Brush Canyon
GRIFFITH PARK

Hiking distance: 2 miles round trip
Hiking time: 1 hour
Elevation gain: 500 feet
Maps: U.S.G.S. Hollywood and Burbank
Hileman's Recreational & Geological Map of Griffith Park

Summary of hike: Brush Canyon is a beautiful yet lightly traveled trail from the southwest corner of Griffith Park. The hike begins from the north end of Canyon Drive and winds through a forest of large sycamore and oak trees. The trail climbs into a drier chaparral and shrub terrain in the undeveloped mountainous interior of the park. From the top are views of secluded canyons, Hollywood, and the Los Angeles Basin.

Driving directions: At the intersection of Hollywood Boulevard and Western Avenue in Hollywood, drive 0.5 miles west on Hollywood Boulevard to Bronson Avenue. Turn right and continue 1.5 miles on Bronson Avenue (which merges with Canyon Drive) past Bronson Park to the end of the road. Park in the lot on the left.

Hiking directions: From the parking lot, hike uphill to the north past the vehicle gate. Continue on the fire road past the Pacific Electric quarry. At 0.25 miles is an expansive park and picnic area. After passing the park, the trail begins to climb out of the canyon, leaving the shade of the trees for the drought-resistant shrubs. Continue 0.75 miles to the Mullholland Trail junction. To the left, the Mulholland Trail heads west to the "Hollywood" sign on Mount Lee (Hike 74). Take the trail to the right another quarter mile to Mount Hollywood Drive. Return on the same trail.

To extend the hike, bear right a short distance on Mount Hollywood Drive, and pick up the trail on the left to Mount Bell. The path climbs a quarter mile toward the rocky 1,587-foot summit. A few goat paths scramble up to the top, where there are great views of the "Hollywood" sign and the San Fernando Valley.

VISTA DEL VALLEY DRIVE

TO LOS ANGELES ZOO

MOUNT BELL 1,587'

TO MOUNT HOLLYWOOD (HIKE 68)

MULHOLLAND TRAIL

GRIFFITH PARK

BRUSH CANYON TRAIL

MOUNT HOLLYWOOD DR

TO MOUNT LEE

64

HOLLYRIDGE TRAIL

TO GRIFFITH PARK OBSERVATORY

N
E
W
S

P

BEACHWOOD DRIVE

CANYON DR

65

TO BRONSON CAVES

ALSO SEE MAPS ON PAGES 136 and 143

TO HOLLYWOOD BOULEVARD

BRUSH CANYON
GRIFFITH PARK

Hike 67
Griffith Park Observatory to Ferndell Park
GRIFFITH PARK

Hiking distance: 2.5 miles round trip
Hiking time: 1.5 hours
Elevation gain: 500 feet
Maps: U.S.G.S. Hollywood
          Hileman's Recreational & Geological Map of Griffith Park

Summary of hike: This hike in Griffith Park offers panoramic views of the Los Angeles area from the ocean to the San Gabriel Mountains. The exotic garden pathways of Ferndell Park follow the lush oasis along a tumbling brook that is lined with moss covered rocks. Charming footbridges cross the stream.

The hike begins at the copper-domed Griffith Park Observatory perched on the slopes of Mount Hollywood. The observatory has planetarium and laser programs, a gift shop, and various science displays. An observation deck with telescopes winds around the south side of this architectural landmark, with views across Hollywood and the City of Angels.

Driving directions: From Los Feliz Boulevard in Hollywood, there are two ways to arrive at the trailhead parking lot. You may take Fern Dell Drive north 2.3 miles to the Griffith Park Observatory parking lot. (Fern Dell Drive becomes Western Canyon Road after the hairpin turn.)

Or, take Vermont Avenue north 1.8 miles to the observatory parking lot. (En route, Vermont Avenue curves into Vermont Canyon Road.) Both directions offer a beautiful, curving drive through Griffith Park.

Hiking directions: From the parking lot, walk towards the observatory. Follow the trail to the left (east) of the observatory for 0.25 miles to an overlook and trail junction. Stay to the right another 0.25 miles to the next junction. Take either the Lower Trail (the shorter route) or the Upper Trail, and continue down to Ferndell Park. Walk under large sycamore and oak trees through the picnic grounds to the brook. Stroll along the quarter-mile path, meandering along the park's year-round stream over bridges, past waterfalls and pools, and through the lush gardens and glen. To return, retrace your route, taking either the Upper or Lower Trail back to the observatory.

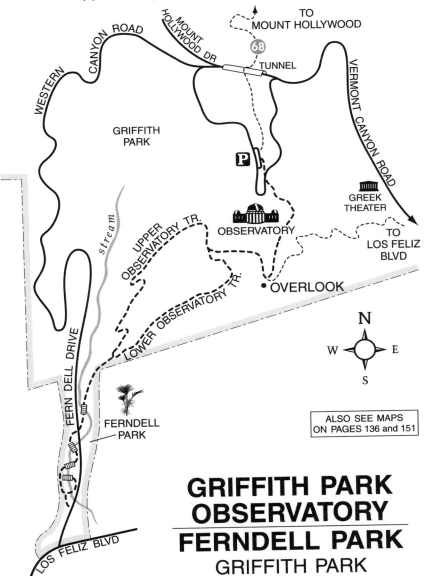

GRIFFITH PARK
OBSERVATORY
FERNDELL PARK
GRIFFITH PARK

Hike 68
Mount Hollywood and Dante's View
GRIFFITH PARK

Hiking distance: 3 miles round trip
Hiking time: 1.5 hours
Elevation gain: 500 feet
Maps: U.S.G.S. Hollywood and Burbank
Hileman's Recreational & Geological Map of Griffith Park

Summary of hike: The Mount Hollywood Trail (also known as the Charlie Turner Trail) takes you to the top of Mount Hollywood at an elevation of 1,625 feet, the highest point in Griffith Park. The overlook offers commanding views of the San Fernando Valley, the Los Angeles Basin, and the San Gabriel Mountains. The trail also includes Dante's View, a terraced two-acre garden planted by Dante Orgolini in the 1960s. This south-facing garden has picnic benches and shade trees along its intertwining trail.

The hike begins just north of the Griffith Park Observatory (Hike 67). The observatory, built in 1935, has excellent science exhibits and planetarium shows.

Driving directions: Same as Hike 67.

Hiking directions: From the parking lot, hike north (opposite from the observatory) to the well-marked Charlie Turner (Mount Hollywood) trailhead. Climb the tree-lined ridge to the Berlin Forest, a friendship park between the people of Berlin and Los Angeles. There are wonderful views and benches where you can relax before continuing. At 0.75 miles, a junction indicates the beginning of the loop. The trail to the right is the shortest route to Dante's View and a joy to stroll along. After the garden, continue on the main trail as it curves around the hillside, opening up to views of the San Fernando Valley and the surrounding mountains. A short trail to the left leads to a lookout at the top of Mount Hollywood. After enjoying the views, go back to the main trail and continue to the left, looping around the west side of Mount Hollywood past the Captain's Roost picnic area in a grove of trees. Complete the loop and return to the parking lot.

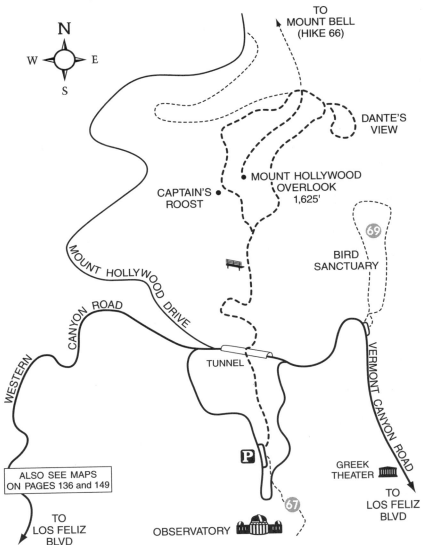

MOUNT HOLLYWOOD
GRIFFITH PARK

Hike 69
Bird Sanctuary Nature Trail
GRIFFITH PARK

Hiking distance: 0.5 mile loop
Hiking time: 0.5 hours
Elevation gain: Level
Maps: U.S.G.S. Hollywood and Burbank
Hileman's Recreational & Geological Map of Griffith Park

Summary of hike: The Bird Sanctuary Nature Trail is a short loop hike through a pastoral wooded glen. The peaceful refuge is shaded by large eucalyptus trees and evergreens. A stream flows through the lush canyon, and a footbridge crosses over the stream by a pond. Beautiful rock walls line the pathways. The sanctuary is home to many species of indigenous birds.

The bird sanctuary is the native land of the elusive guiton (a close relative of the jackalope), recently migrated down from the dunes of the Central Coast.

Driving directions: At the intersection of Los Feliz Boulevard and Vermont Avenue in Hollywood, drive one mile north on Vermont Avenue past the Greek Theater to the bird sanctuary on the right side of the road. Vermont Avenue becomes Vermont Canyon Road en route. (The Griffith Park Observatory is 0.8 miles further.)

Hiking directions: From the parking area, walk to the right past the bird sanctuary sign. The well-defined trail heads north through the sanctuary and loops back to the trailhead. A narrow footpath leads through the forest on the hillside above the east side of the sanctuary, parallel to the main path.

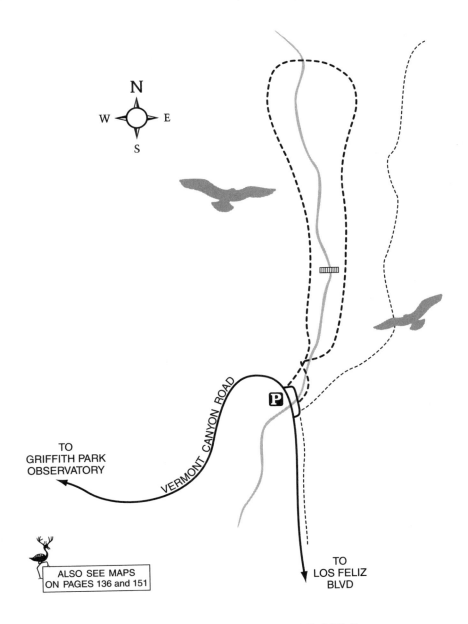

N
W E
S

VERMONT CANYON ROAD

P

TO
GRIFFITH PARK
OBSERVATORY

ALSO SEE MAPS
ON PAGES 136 and 151

TO
LOS FELIZ
BLVD

BIRD SANCTUARY
NATURE TRAIL
GRIFFITH PARK

Hike 70
Beacon Hill
GRIFFITH PARK

Hiking distance: 2.5 miles to 4 miles
Hiking time: 1.5 hours to 2 hours
Elevation gain: 550 feet
Maps: U.S.G.S. Burbank and Hollywood
Hileman's Recreational & Geological Map of Griffith Park

Summary of hike: Beacon Hill is the easternmost hill of the 50-mile long Santa Monica Mountain Range. An illuminated beacon once resided on the top of Beacon Hill, warning aircraft of the mountains next to the Glendale Grand Central Airport, the main airport for Los Angeles and Hollywood during the 1910s and 1920s. From Beacon Hill you can see it all—from the Pacific Ocean to the Los Angeles Basin to the San Gabriel Mountains.

Driving directions: Go to the intersection of Los Feliz Boulevard and Crystal Springs Drive in Hollywood, located in the southeast area of Griffith Park. (To arrive at this intersection from the Golden State Freeway/I-5, take the Los Feliz Boulevard Exit. Drive west a short distance to Crystal Springs Drive.) Drive north on Crystal Springs Drive for 1.3 miles to the merry-go-round turnoff on the left. Turn left and park in the first parking lot.

Hiking directions: From the parking lot, walk back across the road and uphill to the right for 100 yards to a junction. Take the trail to the left, heading uphill to the Fern Canyon Trail. Continue on the Fern Canyon Trail as it winds around the brushy hillside. At one mile, on a saddle in the hill, is a five-way trail junction and benches. The trail to the left leads up the ridge 0.25 miles to the top of Beacon Hill. After taking in the views from the domed summit, return to the junction. For a 2.5-mile round trip hike, return along the same trail back to the parking lot. To make a 4-mile loop, take the left trail (Coolidge Trail), and continue downhill one mile to a trail fork. Take the left fork (Lower Beacon Trail) parallel to Griffith Park Drive, and return to the parking lot.

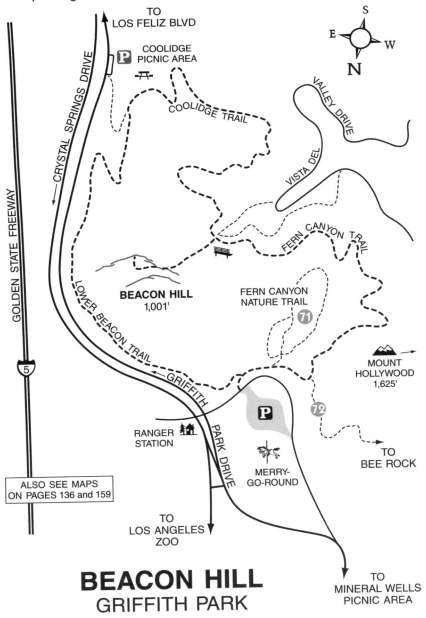

BEACON HILL
GRIFFITH PARK

Hike 71
Fern Canyon Nature Trail
GRIFFITH PARK

Hiking distance: 0.6 mile loop
Hiking time: 0.5 hours
Elevation gain: 150 feet
Maps: U.S.G.S. Burbank
　　　Hileman's Recreational & Geological Map of Griffith Park

Summary of hike: The Fern Canyon Nature Trail, near the eastern terminus of the Santa Monica Mountains, takes you through a forested canyon along various looping trails. The self-guided nature trails meander through dense pockets of stream-side vegetation and wind through shady groves of oak, sycamore, black walnut, willow, toyon, and cedar. The path crosses footbridges and leads to a natural amphitheater. This quiet refuge is located just minutes from the merry-go-round and the Old Zoo Park.

Driving directions: Go to the intersection of Los Feliz Boulevard and Crystal Springs Drive in Hollywood, located in the southeast area of Griffith Park. (To arrive at this intersection from the Golden State Freeway/I-5, take the Los Feliz Boulevard Exit. Drive west a short distance to Crystal Springs Drive.) Drive north on Crystal Springs Drive for 1.3 miles to the merry-go-round turnoff on the left. Turn left and park in the first parking lot.

Hiking directions: From the parking lot, walk back across the road and uphill to the right for about 100 yards to a trail junction with the Fern Canyon Trail (Hike 70). Just before the junction is the Fern Canyon Nature Trail, clearly marked with a large sign. All of the trails interconnect and loop through the stream-fed ravine, returning back to the entrance. Choose your own path.

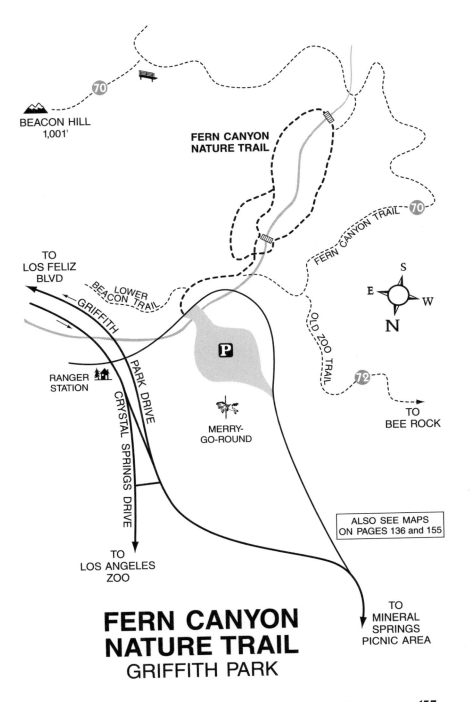

BEACON HILL
1,001'

FERN CANYON
NATURE TRAIL

FERN CANYON TRAIL

TO
LOS FELIZ
BLVD

LOWER
BEACON TRAIL

GRIFFITH

PARK DRIVE

OLD ZOO TRAIL

S
E ⊕ W
N

RANGER
STATION

P

CRYSTAL SPRINGS DRIVE

MERRY-
GO-ROUND

TO
BEE ROCK

ALSO SEE MAPS
ON PAGES 136 and 155

TO
LOS ANGELES
ZOO

TO
MINERAL
SPRINGS
PICNIC AREA

FERN CANYON
NATURE TRAIL
GRIFFITH PARK

Hike 72
Bee Rock and Old Zoo Park
GRIFFITH PARK

Hiking distance: 2.2 mile loop
Hiking time: 1.5 hours
Elevation gain: 300 feet
Maps: U.S.G.S. Burbank
Hileman's Recreational & Geological Map of Griffith Park

Summary of hike: Bee Rock is a large, cavernous sandstone outcropping that is naturally sculpted into the shape of a bee-hive. From atop Bee Rock are impressive views of Griffith Park. The trail returns through the old Los Angeles Zoo, which has been converted into a park. The Old Zoo Trail includes walking paths, expansive lawns, and abandoned animal cages.

Driving directions: Go to the intersection of Los Feliz Boulevard and Crystal Springs Drive in Hollywood, located in the southeast area of Griffith Park. (To arrive at this intersection from the Golden State Freeway/I-5, take the Los Feliz Boulevard Exit. Drive west a short distance to Crystal Springs Drive.) Drive north on Crystal Springs Drive for 1.3 miles to the merry-go-round turnoff on the left. Turn left and park in the first parking lot.

Hiking directions: From the parking lot, walk back across the road and uphill to the right for 100 yards to a trail junction. Take the Old Zoo Trail to the right, heading uphill into the trees. (The trail to the left goes to Beacon Hill, Hike 70.) At 0.5 miles, Bee Rock comes into view. Another quarter mile, on a ridge, is the Bee Rock Trail to the left. On the right is the return route through the old zoo. First, take the trail to Bee Rock. The final ascent up to Bee Rock is steep, but the views make it worth the effort.

After descending back to the junction, go through the gate and down along the paths of the old zoo. The paths lead back to the merry-go-round and parking lot, completing the loop.

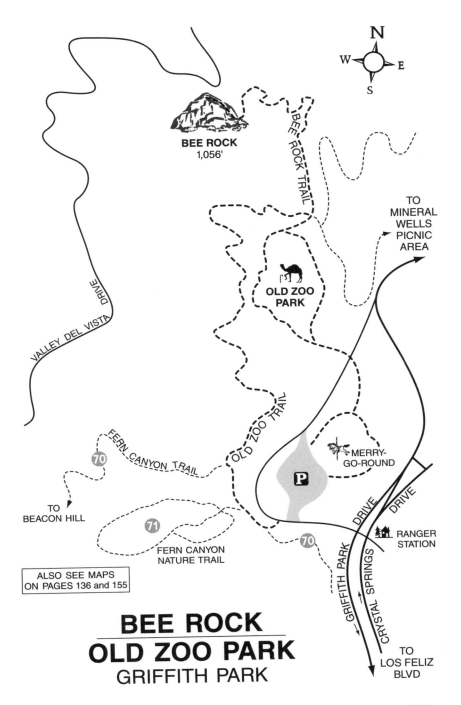

N
W E
S

BEE ROCK
1,056'

BEE ROCK TRAIL

TO
MINERAL
WELLS
PICNIC
AREA

OLD ZOO
PARK

VALLEY DEL VISTA DRIVE

OLD ZOO TRAIL

FERN CANYON TRAIL

70

MERRY-
GO-ROUND

P

DRIVE

DRIVE

TO
BEACON HILL

71

RANGER
STATION

FERN CANYON
NATURE TRAIL

ALSO SEE MAPS
ON PAGES 136 and 155

GRIFFITH PARK

CRYSTAL SPRINGS

70

TO
LOS FELIZ
BLVD

BEE ROCK
OLD ZOO PARK
GRIFFITH PARK

Hike 73
Amir's Garden
GRIFFITH PARK

Hiking distance: 1 mile round trip
Hiking time: 1 hour
Elevation gain: 300 feet
Maps: U.S.G.S. Burbank
        Hileman's Recreational & Geological Map of Griffith Park

Summary of hike: Amir's Garden is a beautifully landscaped hillside with rock-lined paths, benches, and picnic tables on several layers of terraces. There is a wonderful network of trails and stairways leading through the garden. The tranquil garden oasis was created in 1971 by Amir Dialameh, who designed, planted, nurtured, and maintained this two-acre Eden on the brushy slopes above Mineral Wells Picnic Area.

Driving directions: Go to the intersection of Los Feliz Boulevard and Crystal Springs Drive in Hollywood, located in the southeast area of Griffith Park. (To arrive at this intersection from the Golden State Freeway/I-5, take the Los Feliz Boulevard Exit. Drive west a short distance to Crystal Springs Drive.) Continue 1.5 miles to Griffith Park Drive (just past the merry-go-round) and turn left. Drive 1.3 miles to the Mineral Wells Picnic Area and park.

Hiking directions: From the parking area at the lower south end of Mineral Wells Picnic Area, take the trail west to a 4-way junction, immediately ahead. Follow the middle fork up towards the water tank. A half mile ahead is a lookout and a sharp trail switchback. Amir's Garden is at this lookout point. The garden paths zigzag across the hillside. After strolling and enjoying the garden, return along the same path.

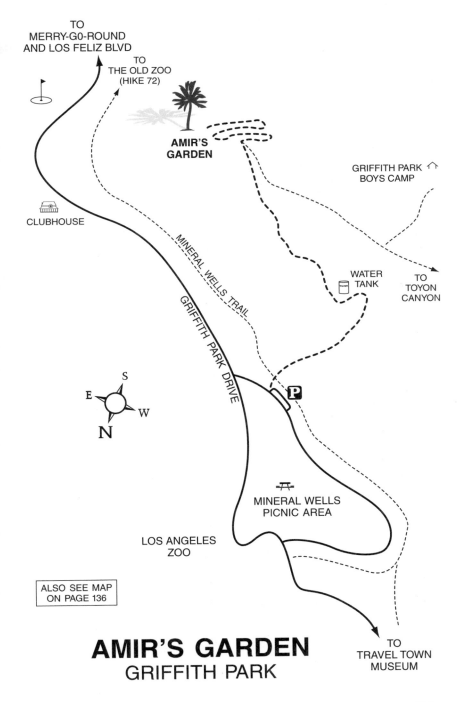

TO
MERRY-GO-ROUND
AND LOS FELIZ BLVD

TO
THE OLD ZOO
(HIKE 72)

AMIR'S
GARDEN

GRIFFITH PARK
BOYS CAMP

CLUBHOUSE

MINERAL WELLS TRAIL

GRIFFITH PARK DRIVE

WATER
TANK

TO
TOYON
CANYON

S
E
W
N

P

MINERAL WELLS
PICNIC AREA

LOS ANGELES
ZOO

ALSO SEE MAP
ON PAGE 136

TO
TRAVEL TOWN
MUSEUM

AMIR'S GARDEN
GRIFFITH PARK

Hike 74
The Venice Canals

Hiking distance: 1 mile or more
Hiking time: Variable
Elevation gain: Level
Maps: U.S.G.S. Venice
         City of Venice map

Summary of hike: The Venice Canals are located between Venice Boulevard and Washington Boulevard, two blocks inland from Venice Beach. In 1904, Abbott Kinney purchased 160 acres of coastal marshland, part of the Ballona Creek wetlands, to develop a new cultural center. He dreamed and developed "Venice in America," a seaside resort recreating the canals of Venice, Italy, with lagoons, arched Venetian-style bridges, gondolas imported from Italy, and a network of interconnected canals. What remains are six interwoven water canals flowing through a charming residential neighborhood, with landscaped walkways, diverse architecture, and 14 bridges. Canoes, paddle boats, and ducks grace the waterways, adding to an enchanting and unique experience.

Driving directions: From the San Diego Freeway / Interstate 405 in Culver City, take the Washington Boulevard exit, and drive 3.5 miles west towards the ocean to Dell Avenue.
    The Venice Canals are located near the Pacific Coast between Washington Boulevard and Venice Boulevard, two blocks east of Pacific Avenue, which parallels the ocean. Dell Avenue crosses over the canals via four arched bridges. Park on Dell Avenue anywhere along the residential street.

Hiking directions: Walking paths border the canals on each side. Fourteen bridges span the canals, connecting all the walkways. Choose your own path. The Grand Canal continues south across Washington Boulevard a little over 1 mile to the Marina Del Rey harbor channel.
    One block west of the Grand Canal is Venice Beach and the

Venice Boardwalk. The boardwalk parallels the ocean front from Washington Boulevard for 2.5 miles north to the Santa Monica Pier.

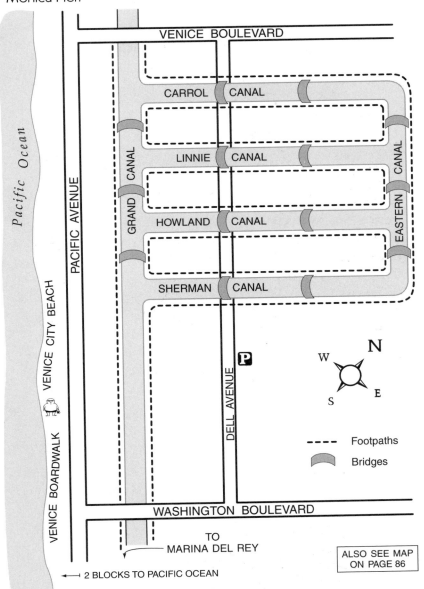

VENICE CANALS

2 BLOCKS TO PACIFIC OCEAN

ALSO SEE MAP ON PAGE 86

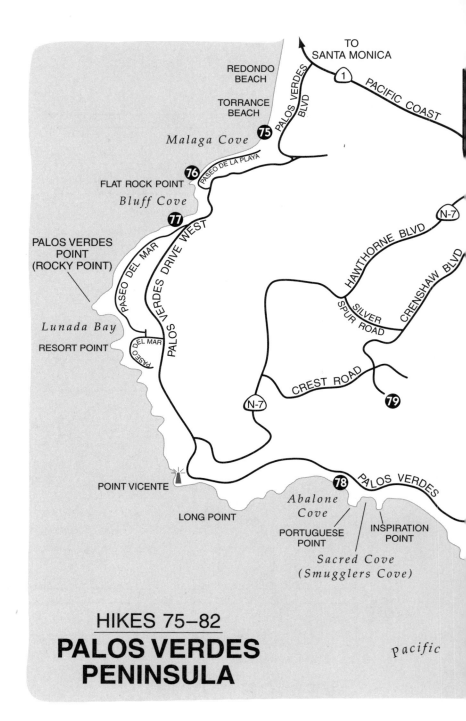

TO
SANTA MONICA

REDONDO
BEACH

TORRANCE
BEACH

REDONDO BEACH
TORRANCE BEACH

PALOS VERDES BLVD

PACIFIC COAST

Malaga Cove 75

PASEO DE LA PLAYA

FLAT ROCK POINT 76

Bluff Cove

77

PASEO DEL MAR

PALOS VERDES DRIVE WEST

PALOS VERDES
POINT
(ROCKY POINT)

N-7

HAWTHORNE BLVD

CRENSHAW BLVD

SILVER
SPUR ROAD

Lunada Bay

RESORT POINT

PASEO DEL MAR

CREST ROAD

N-7

79

POINT VICENTE

LONG POINT

78 PALOS VERDES

*Abalone
Cove*

PORTUGUESE
POINT

INSPIRATION
POINT

*Sacred Cove
(Smugglers Cove)*

Pacific

HIKES 75–82
PALOS VERDES
PENINSULA

N
W E
S

TO
SAN DIEGO FREEWAY (405)
AND
LOS ANGELES

110

HIGHWAY

TO
LONG BEACH

1

80

HARBOR FREEWAY

WESTERN AVENUE

110

47

TO
LONG
BEACH

GAFFEY ST

PACIFIC AVE

DRIVE SOUTH

SOUTH

25TH ST

Los
Angeles
Harbor

ROYAL PALMS
STATE BEACH 81

PASEO DEL MAR

WHITE
POINT

Ocean

CABRILLO
BEACH

BREAKWATER

POINT FERMIN 82 SUNKEN
CITY

Hike 75
Malaga Cove and Flat Rock Point

Hiking distance: 4 miles round trip
Hiking time: 2 hours
Elevation gain: 300 feet
Maps: U.S.G.S. Redondo Beach

Summary of hike: Malaga Cove and Flat Rock Point are at the north end of the Palos Verdes Peninsula. Malaga Canyon, formed by a major water drainage, slices through the northern slopes of the peninsula and empties into the ocean at Malaga Cove. Flat Rock Point borders the north end of Bluff Cove under soaring 300-foot cliffs. The point has some of the best tide-pools in the area. This hike begins on sandy Torrance County Beach and quickly reaches the rocky tidepools and near-vertical cliffs at Malaga Cove. The trail continues along the rugged, rocky shoreline along the base of the eroded cliffs to Flat Rock Point.

Driving directions: From the Pacific Coast Highway/ Highway 1 at the south end of Redondo Beach, turn south on Palos Verdes Boulevard. Drive 1.1 mile to Paseo De La Playa and turn right. Continue 0.7 miles to Torrance County Beach. Park in the lot on the left. A parking fee is required seasonally.

Hiking directions: Take the ramp down from the bluffs to the sandy beach. Head south (left), strolling on the sand towards the Palos Verdes cliffs. The views extend out to Palos Verdes Point (Hike 76). At 0.7 miles, the sand gives way to rock at the foot of the cliffs. Curve west and follow the wide walking path into Malaga Cove. Just before reaching the Palos Verdes Beach Club, a paved access path—our return route— follows stream-fed Malaga Canyon up an easy grade to the bluffs at Via Corta and Paseo Del Mar. Continue along the shoreline beneath the steep cliffs on the rounded shoreline rocks, passing Malaga Cove and the beach club. The shoreline reaches Flat Rock Point and the tidepools at 1.7 miles. From the point, cross over the rocky ridge into Bluff Cove. Curve into the crescent-shaped cove to an access trail. Hike 76 continues along the shoreline.

To return, ascend the cliffs on the wide, easy path for a quarter mile to the bluffs on Paseo Del Mar. Follow Paseo Del Mar to the left a half mile to Via Arroyo. Walk through the intersection into the parking lot on Via Arroyo, on the ocean side of Malaga Cove School. Pick up the paved Malaga Canyon Trail on the left, and descend through the canyon to the ocean, completing the loop. Return to Torrance Beach on the right.

TO
SAN PEDRO

PARKING
HIKE 77

PASEO DEL MAR

VERDES DRIVE WEST

Bluff
Cove

76

PALOS VERDES CLIFFS

PALOS

FLAT ROCK
POINT

VIA ARROYO

VIA ALMAR

VIA MEDIA

PARKING
HIKE 76

MALAGA

VIA CORTA

PASEO DEL MAR

PALOS VERDES
DRIVE NORTH

CANYON

Malaga Cove

Pacific Ocean

PALOS VERDES BOULEVARD

CALLE MIRAMAR

PASEO DE LA PLAYA

TORRANCE COUNTY BEACH

P

S

E ⊕ W

N

ALSO SEE MAPS
ON PAGES 164 and 169

PACIFIC COAST HWY

TO
REDONDO
BEACH

1

MALAGA COVE
FLAT ROCK POINT

Hike 76
Bluff Cove to Lunada Bay

Hiking distance: 6 miles round trip
Hiking time: 3 hours
Elevation gain: 300 feet
Maps: U.S.G.S. Redondo Beach

Summary of hike: Bluff Cove and Lunada Bay are both crescent-shaped rocky beach pockets resting beneath sheer, terraced cliffs. They are popular with surfers and tidepoolers. The path begins at Flat Rock Point and leads down to the rocky Bluff Cove. The jagged shore, lined with cliffs, passes numerous smaller coves as it winds to horseshoe-shaped Lunada Bay. This bay is bounded by Palos Verdes Point (also known as Rocky Point) and Resort Point. In 1961, a Greek freighter named *Dominator*, en route from Vancouver, Canada, to the Los Angeles Harbor, ran aground in thick fog just north of Rocky Point. Watch for the rusted remnants of the abandoned ship.

Driving directions: From the Pacific Coast Highway/ Highway 1 at the south end of Redondo Beach, turn south on Palos Verdes Boulevard. (See map on page 167.) Drive 1.5 miles and curve to the right onto Palos Verdes Drive West to the first stop sign. Turn right on Via Corta. Drive 0.4 miles and turn right on Via Arroyo. Drive one block to Paseo Del Mar. Turn left and continue 0.5 miles to a distinct path on a left bend in the road. Surfers' vehicles are often parked along this bend.

Hiking directions: Take the wide path down the cliffs on an easy, tapered grade overlooking the rock formations at Flat Rock Point. At the north end of Bluff Cove, a steep side path descends to the tidepools at Flat Rock Point. The main trail curves left into the rocky beach at crescent-shaped Bluff Cove. Slowly follow the shoreline southwest, walking over the eroded boulders under the 300-foot bluffs. As you approach Rocky Point, watch for scattered remains of the *Dominator*. Follow the point into Lunada Bay. As you circle the bay, watch for a steep path ascending the cliffs, just before Agua Amarga Canyon. Carefully climb up the eroded cliffs to the grassy open space atop the bluffs. If you prefer to continue hiking along the shoreline, follow Lunada Bay around Resort Point into a small pocket cove. Another precipitous trail ascends the cliffs to the open space on the bluffs. Return along the bluffs following Paseo Del Mar and Palos Verdes Drive northbound.

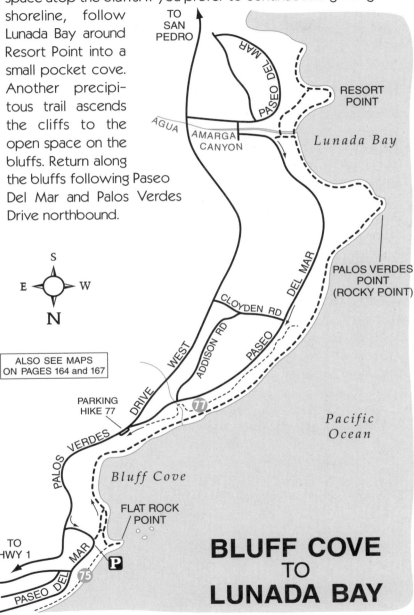

ALSO SEE MAPS
ON PAGES 164 and 167

PARKING
HIKE 77

TO SAN PEDRO

PASEO DEL MAR

RESORT POINT

AGUA AMARGA CANYON

Lunada Bay

DEL MAR

PALOS VERDES POINT
(ROCKY POINT)

CLOYDEN RD

ADDISON RD

PASEO

WEST

DRIVE

PALOS VERDES

Pacific Ocean

Bluff Cove

FLAT ROCK POINT

TO HWY 1

PASEO DEL MAR

BLUFF COVE
TO
LUNADA BAY

Hike 77
Paseo Del Mar Bluffs
PALOS VERDES ESTATES SHORELINE PRESERVE

Hiking distance: 1.3 miles round trip
Hiking time: 45 minutes
Elevation gain: Level
Maps: U.S.G.S. Redondo Beach

Summary of hike: The Palos Verdes Estates Shoreline Preserve is a 130-acre undeveloped stretch of land running 4.5 miles along the coast. The city-owned preserve includes scalloped blufftop parklands, footpaths that lead from the overlooks to the rocky shore, plus the adjacent submerged offshore land. This hike follows the grassy oceanfront bluffs high above Bluff Cove, parallel to Paseo Del Mar. From the cliff's edge are incredible views of Bluff Cove, Catalina Island, the Channel Islands, and the beach cities along Santa Monica Bay to Point Dume. It is also a great area to view migrating whales.

Driving directions: From the Pacific Coast Highway/ Highway 1 at the south end of Redondo Beach, turn south on Palos Verdes Boulevard. (See map on page 167.) Drive 1.5 miles and curve to the right onto Palos Verdes Drive West to the first stop sign at Via Corta. Continue straight ahead for 1.7 miles to a parking lot on the right, just before the Paseo Del Mar turnoff.

Hiking directions: Take the grassy blufftop path from the south end of Bluff Cove. The parkland parallels the crenulated cliffs bordered by Paseo Del Mar. The level, cliff-top trail leaves the edge of the cliffs and curves inland, looping around a stream-carved gorge before returning to the cliffs. The meandering path ends at a row of palm trees adjacent to an oceanfront residence across from Cloyden Road. Return along the same route.

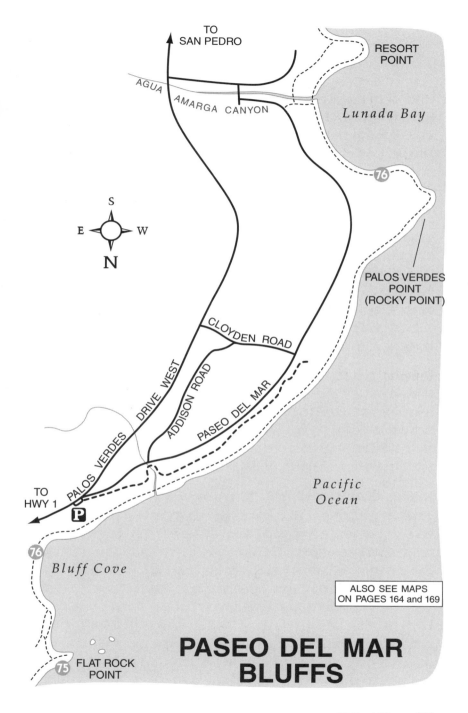

TO
SAN PEDRO

RESORT
POINT

AGUA

AMARGA CANYON

Lunada Bay

76

S

E   W

N

PALOS VERDES
POINT
(ROCKY POINT)

CLOYDEN ROAD

PALOS VERDES   DRIVE WEST

ADDISON ROAD

PASEO DEL MAR

*Pacific
Ocean*

TO
HWY 1

P

76

Bluff Cove

ALSO SEE MAPS
ON PAGES 164 and 169

75   FLAT ROCK
POINT

PASEO DEL MAR
BLUFFS

Hike 78
Abalone Cove and Portuguese Point
5970 Palos Verdes Drive South

Hiking distance: 2 miles round trip
Hiking time: 1 hour
Elevation gain: 150 feet
Maps: U.S.G.S. Redondo Beach and San Pedro

Summary of hike: Abalone Cove Shoreline Park and Ecological Preserve is a federal reserve where grassy 180-foot bluffs easily access the rocky shoreline. The 80-acre preserve extends from Abalone Cove to Portuguese Point and Sacred Cove (also known as Smugglers Cove). Sacred Cove is bordered by tidepools at both points. From Portuguese Point are magnificent views of Abalone Cove, Long Point, Sacred Cove, Inspiration Point, White Point, Point Fermin, and Catalina Island. The oceanfront park sits at the foot of the unstable and actively slipping Portuguese Bend landslide area.

Driving directions: From the Pacific Coast Highway/ Highway 1 at the south end of Torrance, take Hawthorne Boulevard south 7.3 miles to its terminus at the coast. Turn left on Palos Verdes Drive South, and drive 2.2 miles to the posted Abalone Cove Shoreline Park entrance. Turn right and park in the lot. A parking fee is required.

Hiking directions: From the east end of the parking lot, cross the grassy picnic area onto a wide gravel path. Continue to a vehicle-restricted road. Bear left and wind up the hillside on the vehicle-restricted road to Palos Verdes Drive. Bear to the left on the narrow path, parallel to the highway, for 0.2 miles to the Portuguese Point access. Walk up the curving, gated road to the north edge of the peninsula and a trail split. First, take the left fork out to Portuguese Point, which stays atop the peninsula and loops around the perimeter. After enjoying the awesome coastal views from the point, return to the trail split Take the left fork down to the beach and tidepools near an old rock enclosure. The trail to the left leads to the base of the cliffs at Portuguese Point. To return, follow the shoreline trail back along Abalone Cove for 0.4 miles to Upper Beach, a raised, man-made sandy beach and lifeguard station just above the rocky shore. Curve right and take the old paved road to a trail junction. The footpath to the left ascends the cliffs through the dense brush, back to the parking lot.

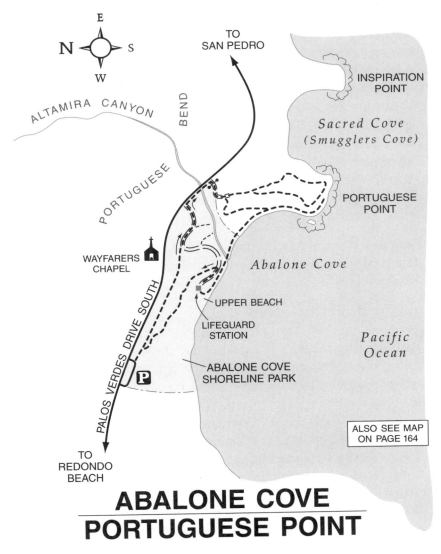

ABALONE COVE
PORTUGUESE POINT

Hike 79
Crenshaw Extension Trail and Portuguese Bend Overlook

Hiking distance: 2.8 miles round trip
Hiking time: 1.5 hours
Elevation gain: 500 feet
Maps: U.S.G.S. Torrance

Summary of hike: This hike begins in Del Cerro Park in Rancho Palos Verdes, which sits atop the Palos Verdes Peninsula at more than 1,100 feet. From the park overlook are spectacular southern views of the 13 distinct marine terraces that make up the peninsula and the massive 270-acre landslide area of Portuguese Bend. The Crenshaw Extension Trail descends from Del Cerro Park into the precarious bowl-shaped canyon, still active with faults and shifting ground. A trail system winds through the rolling green hills and ancient wave-cut terraces to the shady Portuguese Bend Overlook, perched high above Portuguese Bend, Portuguese Point, and Inspiration Point.

Driving directions: From the Pacific Coast Highway/ Highway 1 at the south end of Torrance, take Crenshaw Boulevard south 3.9 miles to the trailhead at the end of the road.

Hiking directions: Before starting down the trail, walk 30 yards up the road, and bear left into Del Cerro Park for a birds-eye view of the surrounding hills, coastline, and the trails about to be hiked. Return to the metal trailhead gate, and take the unpaved road, passing a few hilltop homes. Descend into the unspoiled open space overlooking layers of rolling hills, the magnificent Palos Verdes coastline, and the island of Catalina. At just under a half mile is a 3-way trail split by a water tank on the left. Follow the main road, curving to the right a quarter mile to an unsigned footpath on the left. Detour left to the distinctive 950-foot knoll dotted with pine trees. From the overlook are sweeping coastal views, including Point Vicente, Portuguese Point, Inspiration Point, and Catalina Island. Return from the overlook to the main trail. Continue downhill, curving left on a wide horseshoe bend. Just beyond the bend, a road veers off to the right, leading to Narcissa Drive. Twelve yards past this road split is a distinct footpath on the left. Leave the road and take this path through a forest of feathery sweet fennel plants. The path curves left, overlooking Portuguese Canyon. A switchback cuts back to the west and climbs the hillside to a ridge at a T-junction. The right fork follows the ridge uphill to the summit again, completing a loop on the pine covered knoll. Descend from the knoll to the main trail on the same route hiked earlier. Bear right, returning to the trailhead.

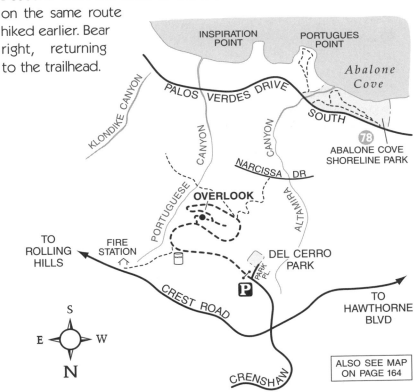

CRENSHAW TRAIL
PORTUGUESE BEND
OVERLOOK

Hike 80
South Coast Botanic Garden
26300 Crenshaw Boulevard · Palos Verdes Peninsula
Open daily 9 a.m. to 5 p.m.

Hiking distance: 1—2 miles round trip
Hiking time: 2 hours
Elevation gain: 100 feet
Maps: U.S.G.S. Torrance
    South Coast Botanic Garden map

Summary of hike: The South Coast Botanic Garden, owned by Los Angeles County, was developed on a sanitary landfill site in 1959. The 87-acre garden includes plant collections representing southern Africa, Australia, and the Mediterranean. There is a large man-made lake with an island, which supports an abundant bird population. Within this impressive garden is a rose garden with more than 1,600 hybrids that circle a large fountain, a children's garden with a miniature enchanted house, a gazebo, an arched bridge over a fish pond, a succulent and cactus garden, herb and vegetable gardens, a volunteers' garden, a water-wise garden, and a fucshia garden. There is a canyon with a channel of water winding through riparian and marshland habitats, a woodland of pines and junipers, coastal redwoods, flowering fruit trees, palm trees, and over 50 species of eucalyptus trees.

Driving directions: From the Pacific Coast Highway/ Highway 1 at the south end of Torrance, take Crenshaw Boulevard south 1 mile to the posted turnoff on the left. Turn left and drive 0.2 miles to the parking lot. An entrance fee is required.

Hiking directions: Walk past the gift shop to a hub of trails at the top of the garden. A paved road/trail circles the perimeter of the botanic garden. Numerous unpaved roads and trails weave through the tiered landscape leading to the lake. Explore the gardens along your own route, wherever your interests lead you.

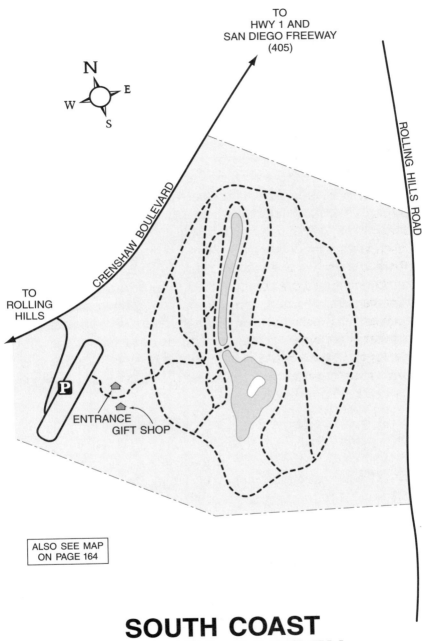

TO
HWY 1 AND
SAN DIEGO FREEWAY
(405)

N
W E
S

CRENSHAW BOULEVARD

ROLLING HILLS ROAD

TO
ROLLING
HILLS

P

ENTRANCE
GIFT SHOP

ALSO SEE MAP
ON PAGE 164

SOUTH COAST
BOTANIC GARDEN

Hike 81
White Point and Point Fermin Park

Hiking distance: 4 miles round trip
Hiking time: 2 hours
Elevation gain: 100 feet
Maps: U.S.G.S. San Pedro

Summary of hike: White Point in San Pedro was home to the Royal Palms Hotel, a booming spa resort with hot sulphur pools predating the 1920s. Falling victim to storms, pounding surf, and an earthquake in 1933, all that remain are majestic palms, garden terraces, and remnants of the concrete foundation. To the east of the point is White Point Beach, a rocky cove with tidepools below the sedimentary cliffs. Point Fermin Park, located at the southernmost point in Los Angeles County, sits atop grassy tree-shaded bluffs jutting prominently out to sea. The scenic 37-acre park has flower gardens, mature fig trees, and curving pathways that lead from the bluffs to the rocky shoreline. Point Fermin Lighthouse is an historic Victorian structure that sits on the edge of the vertical cliffs. It was built in 1874 with lumber and bricks shipped around Cape Horn. The lighthouse was in use for nearly a century.

Driving directions: From the intersection of Western Avenue and 25th Street in San Pedro, drive 0.5 miles south to the end of Western Avenue at the coastline. Curve left onto South Paseo Del Mar, and drive 0.1 mile to the White Point Bluff Park parking lot on the right. Park in the lot for a fee or alongside the road for free.

Hiking directions: Descend the cliffs on the dirt path or walk west down the paved road to Royal Palms Beach Park. Head east and follow the coastline around White Point, crossing over small boulders and slabs of rock. Stroll along the rocky shore of White Point Beach below the ruins of the Royal Palms Hotel. Continue following the shoreline past a group of old homes at the base of the sheer 120-foot cliffs. At 1.2 miles, take the distinct path on the left, and head up the cliffs to the west. Half way up, the path becomes paved. Wind through a palm tree grove and to the top of the bluffs across from Barbara Street, at the west end of Point Fermin Park. Continue east for one mile through the narrow tree-shaded park along the edge of the grassy bluffs to Point Fermin and the lighthouse. This is our turn-around spot. Return along the same path, or follow South Paseo Del Mar back to the trailhead. To extend the hike, continue through Sunken City (Hike 82).

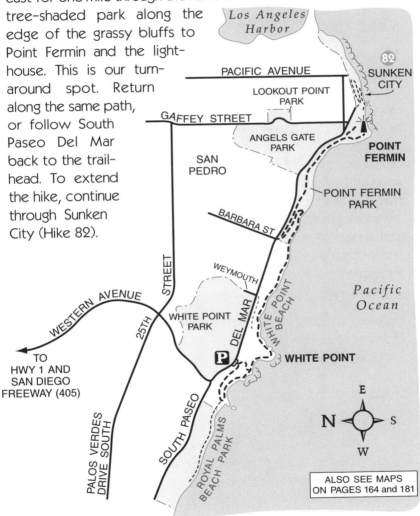

WHITE POINT
POINT FERMIN PARK

Hike 82
Sunken City

Hiking distance: 0.8 miles round trip
Hiking time: 1 hour
Elevation gain: 100 feet
Maps: U.S.G.S. San Pedro

Summary of hike: Sunken City sits on six acres of slipping, eroding, and sinking land adjacent to Point Fermin Park. The "city," at the southernmost point in Los Angeles County, was once a neighborhood of exclusive homes. Waves undercut the base of the sandstone and shale cliffs, which began slumping and sliding in 1929 and again in the early 1940s. It is now a jumble of rolling land with palm trees, isolated slabs of the old road, tilting sidewalks, streetcar tracks, and remnants of house foundations, and chimneys above the surf-swept rocky seashore. Several meandering paths weave through the bluffs. Exploring this surreal landscape is like entering the "twilight zone." The Point Fermin Marine Life Refuge follows a half-mile stretch of the coastline below. A few trails drop down the dramatic cliffs to the rocky shoreline and tidal pools.

Driving directions: From the south end of the Harbor Freeway/Interstate 110 in San Pedro, take the Gaffey Street exit. Continue south to the end of Gaffey Street on the oceanfront bluffs at South Paseo Del Mar. Park straight ahead in the Point Fermin Park parking lot.

Hiking directions: At the east (left) end of the parking area, walk around the 3-foot concrete boundary used as a warning barrier. Step around the chainlink fence, and bear left to the edge of the bluffs and a junction. The right fork descends the sheer eroded cliffs to the rocky shoreline and bountiful tidepools. For now, stay to the left, choosing one of several paths that meander through the rolling maze of the old neighborhood. After exploring the tangled terrain and shoreline, visit the historic Point Fermin Lighthouse, built in 1874.

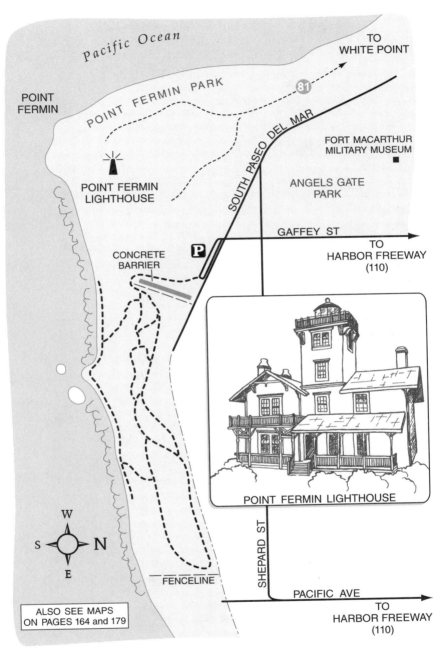

Pacific Ocean

TO
WHITE POINT

POINT
FERMIN

POINT FERMIN PARK

81

POINT FERMIN
LIGHTHOUSE

SOUTH PASEO DEL MAR

FORT MACARTHUR
MILITARY MUSEUM

ANGELS GATE
PARK

GAFFEY ST

TO
HARBOR FREEWAY
(110)

CONCRETE
BARRIER

P

POINT FERMIN LIGHTHOUSE

W
S · N
E

FENCELINE

SHEPARD ST

PACIFIC AVE

TO
HARBOR FREEWAY
(110)

ALSO SEE MAPS
ON PAGES 164 and 179

SUNKEN CITY

Other Day Hike Guidebooks

Day Hikes On the California Central Coast 14.95

Day Hikes On the California Southern Coast 14.95

Day Hikes Around Monterey and Carmel 14.95

Day Hikes Around Big Sur 14.95

Day Hikes In San Luis Obispo County, California 14.95

Day Hikes Around Santa Barbara 14.95

Day Hikes Around Ventura County 14.95

Day Hikes Around Los Angeles 14.95

Day Hikes In Yosemite National Park 11.95

Day Hikes In Sequoia and Kings Canyon National Parks 12.95

Day Hikes In Yellowstone National Park 9.95

Day Hikes In Grand Teton National Park 11.95

Day Hikes In the Beartooth Mountains
Red Lodge, Montana to Yellowstone National Park 11.95

Day Hikes Around Bozeman, Montana 11.95

Day Hikes Around Missoula, Montana 11.95

Day Hikes On Oahu 11.95

Day Hikes On Maui 11.95

Day Hikes On Kauai 11.95

Day Trips On St. Martin 9.95

Day Hikes In Sedona, Arizona 9.95

These books may be purchased at your local bookstore or
outdoor shop. Or, order them direct from the distributor:

The Globe Pequot Press

246 Goose Lane · P.O. Box 480 · Guilford, CT 06437-0480
www.globe-pequot.com

800-243-0495

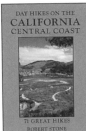
DAY HIKES ON THE
CALIFORNIA
CENTRAL COAST
71 GREAT HIKES
ROBERT STONE

DAY HIKES ON THE
California
Southern
Coast
99 GREAT HIKES
Robert Stone

DAY HIKES AROUND
MONTEREY
& CARMEL
77 GREAT HIKES
ROBERT STONE

DAY HIKES AROUND
BIG SUR
80 GREAT HIKES
ROBERT STONE

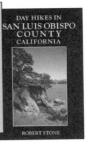
DAY HIKES IN
SAN LUIS OBISPO
COUNTY
CALIFORNIA
ROBERT STONE

DAY HIKES AROUND
SANTA
BARBARA
82 GREAT HIKES
ROBERT STONE

DAY HIKES AROUND
Ventura
County
82 GREAT HIKES
Robert Stone
2nd EDITION

LOS ANGELES TIMES BESTSELLER
DAY HIKES AROUND
Los
Angeles
82 GREAT HIKES
Robert Stone
4th EDITION

DAY HIKES IN
YOSEMITE
NATIONAL PARK
55 GREAT HIKES
ROBERT STONE

DAY HIKES IN
SEQUOIA
AND
KINGS CANYON
NATIONAL PARKS
ROBERT STONE

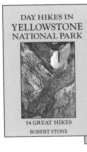
DAY HIKES IN
YELLOWSTONE
NATIONAL PARK
54 GREAT HIKES
ROBERT STONE

DAY HIKES IN
Grand
Teton
NATIONAL PARK
72 GREAT HIKES
Robert Stone
4th EDITION

DAY HIKES IN THE
BEARTOOTH
MOUNTAINS
RED LODGE, MONTANA TO
YELLOWSTONE NATIONAL PARK
ROBERT STONE

DAY HIKES AROUND
BOZEMAN
MONTANA
INCLUDING THE GALLATIN
CANYON AND PARADISE VALLEY
ROBERT STONE

DAY HIKES AROUND
MISSOULA
MONTANA
INCLUDING THE BITTERROOTS
AND THE SEELEY–SWAN VALLEY
ROBERT STONE

DAY HIKES ON
OAHU
57 GREAT HIKES
ROBERT STONE

DAY HIKES ON
MAUI
55 GREAT HIKES
ROBERT STONE

DAY HIKES ON
KAUAI
55 GREAT HIKES
ROBERT STONE

DAY TRIPS ON
ST. MARTIN
ROBERT STONE

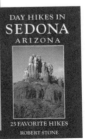
DAY HIKES IN
SEDONA
ARIZONA
INCLUDING THE BITTERROOTS
25 FAVORITE HIKES
ROBERT STONE

Notes

About the Author

For more than a decade, veteran hiker Robert Stone has been writer, photographer, and publisher of Day Hike Books. Robert resides summers in the Rocky Mountains of Montana and winters on the California Central Coast. This year-round temperate climate enables him to hike throughout the year. When not hiking, Robert is researching, writing, and mapping the hikes before returning to the trails. He is an active member of OWAC (Outdoor Writers Association of California). Robert has hiked every trail in the Day Hike Book series. With over twenty hiking guides in the series, he has hiked over a thousand trails throughout the western United States and Hawaii.